Kids' TRAVEL GUIDE TO THE FRUIT OF THE SPIRIT

Group

Loveland, Colorado

Group resources actually work!

This Group resource incorporates our R.E.A.L. approach to ministry. It reinforces a growing friendship with Jesus, encourages long-term learning, and results in life transformation, because it's

Relational

Learner-to-learner interaction enhances learning and builds Christian friendships.

Experiential

What learners experience through discussion and action sticks with them up to 9 times longer than what they simply hear or read.

Applicable

The aim of Christian education is to equip learners to be both hearers and doers of God's Word.

Learner-based

Learners understand and retain more when the learning process takes into consideration how they learn best.

Kids' Travel Guide to the Fruit of the Spirit

Copyright © 2002 Group Publishing, Inc.

Visit our website: **group.com**

Credits

Contributing Authors: Ruthie Daniels, Heather A. Eades, Sara K. Elder, Julie Lavender, Carolyn Luengen, Jennifer Nystrom, and Larry Shallenberger
Editors: Donna Simcoe and Jim Hawley
Creative Development Editor: Karl Leuthauser
Chief Creative Officer: Joani Schultz
Copy Editor: Betty Taylor
Art Director: Kari K. Monson
Computer Graphic Artist: Stephen Beer
Illustrator: Steve Duffendack
Cover Art Director/Designer: Bambi Morehead
Cover Illustrator: Garry Colby
Production Manager: Peggy Naylor

Library of Congress Cataloging-in-Publication Data
Kids' travel guide to the fruits of the Spirit.
   p. cm.
   ISBN 978-0-7644-2390-1 (pbk. : alk. paper)
 1. Fruit of the Spirit. I. Group Publishing.
  BV4501.3 .K53 2002
  268'.432--dc21

                      2002001828

25 24 23 22 21   18 17 16 15 14
Printed in the United States of America.

Table of Contents

An Introduction to the Travel Guide 5

Journey 1 7
What Is the Fruit of the Spirit?

Journey 2 20
Love

Journey 3 28
Joy

Journey 4 35
Peace

Journey 5 43
Patience

Journey 6 52
Kindness

Journey 7 60
Goodness

Journey 8　68
Faithfulness

Journey 9　76
Gentleness

Journey 10　86
Self-Control

Journey 11　94
What It Means to Belong to Jesus

Journey 12　101
Living by the Spirit

Journey 13　111
Staying With or Straying From the Spirit

Kids' Travel Guide

An Introduction to the Travel Guide

This book is designed to help children in kindergarten through fifth grade grow the fruit of the Spirit in their daily lives. Following an overview of the fruit of the Spirit, the lessons each explore one of the nine qualities of the Spirit. The remaining lessons look at how having a relationship with Jesus will help children demonstrate the fruit of the Spirit in their lives.

During this thirteen-week course, each child will complete a **Travel Journal.** The Travel Journal will serve as a keepsake so that the qualities of God's Spirit become written upon kids' hearts and lived out in their everyday experiences.

The **Pathway Point** is the central concept that children will explore and apply to their lives. The **In-Focus Verse** is a Bible verse that summarizes the fruit of the Spirit point of the lesson. A **Travel Itinerary** introduces the lesson and explains how the lesson will impact your kids' lives.

Please read each lesson thoroughly, and make a model for each craft before class. If you do, your lessons will flow much more smoothly. The time recommendations are only guidelines. They will change according to how many are in your group, how prepared you are, and how much help you have.

Each lesson starts with a **Departure Prayer.** These are creative prayer activities that help introduce the topic and focus children on God. **Tour-Guide Tips** are helps for the teacher, and **Scenic Routes** provide more creative options.

First-Stop Discoveries introduce children to the concepts behind God's commandments. The **Story Excursions** are Bible stories that illustrate the Holy Spirit quality being explored. Kids will experience these stories in creative ways, and the stories will give your class variety. Choose what you think will best meet your children's needs. The activities in **Adventures in Growing** lead children to further application of the point. Each week, ask children how God's Spirit helped them live. This will be an important faith-growing time.

Souvenirs are paper activities that can go into the children's Travel Journals. Each lesson closes with a **Home Again Prayer.** These prayers offer a time of commitment and a time to ask for God's Spirit to live in kids' lives.

Any time during a lesson you can, read the **Fun Facts** section to kids. These provide examples of the lesson's point from familiar and not-so-familiar facts.

Exploring the qualities of the fruit of the Spirit will be a blessing to teachers and children alike. May God bless you as you help children "live by the Spirit" (Galatians 5:25a).

What Is the Fruit of the Spirit?

Pathway Point: ⏺ God gives us the fruit of the Spirit to help us show others what his love looks like.

In-Focus Verse: "But the fruit of the Spirit is love, joy, peace, patience, kindness, goodness, faithfulness, gentleness and self-control" (Galatians 5:22-23a).

Travel Itinerary

The fruit of the Spirit is a gift God gives Christians to help them live lives that please him and show his love to those who don't know God. As children learn about the fruit of the spirit, they will learn that God uses us as his instruments to show his love to others! Jesus was the ultimate expression of God's love, and all the qualities of God that made Jesus who he was—love, joy, peace, patience, kindness, goodness, faithfulness, gentleness, and self-control—become qualities in us the closer we grow in our relationships with Jesus.

Younger children are still learning about who Jesus is and will discover in this journey what each fruit of the Spirit looks like. They will learn how to recognize qualities of the fruit of the spirit when they see them.

Older children will discover how to grow and nurture the fruit of the Spirit in their lives and realize the importance of each quality. All children will understand that the fruit of the Spirit is given to us as a tool, equipping us to show God's love to those around us, fulfilling God's commands.

Items to Pack: Bibles

DEPARTURE PRAYER	(5 minutes)

Introduce the nine qualities of the fruit of the Spirit through this prayer. Have children form a circle, and have children number off, one through nine. Repeat the numbering if you have more than nine kids. It isn't necessary for the numbers to come out even. Give each child a Bible, and have kids locate Galatians 5:22-23a. Explain that you'll go around the circle and after you pause, the child who called out number one will say aloud the first quality (love) of the fruit of the Spirit. Continue around the circle, pausing for children to say the remaining eight qualities of the Spirit.

Say: **Heavenly Father, thank you for giving us the fruit of the Spirit. We ask you to help us live each quality of the fruit of the Spirit. Help us to show** [pause for child to say "love"] **and** [joy]. **Help us to have** [peace] **and**

TOUR GUIDE TIP — If you have younger children, they may have difficulty saying their prayer words during your pauses. You could modify the instructions by telling kids that you'll say each fruit of the Spirit quality, and then have each child repeat his or her word after you say it. For example, when you say, "Help us to show love," you'll pause for the child who called out number one to repeat the word "love," and so on with the remaining eight qualities.

show [patience] and [goodness]. **Help us demonstrate [faithfulness] and [gentleness], and finally help us have [self-control]. Please help us show others your love by teaching us your ways and growing us as your children. Please help us, Lord, to show love, joy, peace, patience, kindness, goodness, faithfulness, gentleness, and self-control in the various situations you put us in. Help us to use the fruit of the Spirit to show others what your love looks like. In Jesus' name, amen.**

(15 minutes)
Fruit Filling

This activity demonstrates to kids how Christ's character traits grow inside them as they grow closer in their relationships with God.

Spread out two large sheets of butcher paper, and choose a tall child to lie down, arms at his or her sides, on one of the sheets. Choose a smaller child to lie down, with arms extended overhead, on the other sheet of paper. Have the rest of the students trace around the two children on the paper. Attach both tracings, side by side, to a wall. Explain that the smaller child's outline represents each of us and the taller child's outline represents Jesus.

Stand in front of the two body outlines and say: **We're going to spend some time learning about gifts from God called "fruit of the Spirit." But first we need to understand what fruit of the Spirit is! What do you think of when you hear that term, "fruit of the Spirit"?** Allow children to guess. Say: **Those are all good answers! These gifts, called the fruit of the Spirit, are seeds God grows inside of us to show others what his love looks like. They are seeds of love, joy, peace, patience, kindness, goodness, faithfulness, gentleness, and self-control. All are things Jesus modeled for us to show us what it looks like to show love, to have joy, to be patient, and so on. And the cool thing is, when we accept Jesus to become Lord of our lives, God plants those seeds and they begin to grow! Think about how each of those things shows up in your life. Are you patient when you have to wait your turn in line? Do you show love to people who may not be so easy to love sometimes? Let's think of some ways that we show those gifts right now in our lives.**

Before children arrive, cut out enough fruit shapes from construction paper for each child to have two. Write one gift of the fruit of the Spirit on each cutout, such as "love" or "kindness." Set out markers for children to share. Have each child read which quality of the fruit of the Spirit is written on his or her cutout. Have older children assist younger children with reading. Encourage kids to write

Items to Pack: two large sheets of butcher paper, markers, scissors, masking tape, construction paper fruit shapes, Bible

FUN FACT

Often when people think of growing fruit, they think they need a big yard and big trees. But now scientists have developed dwarf trees, which are miniature fruit trees that grow the same size fruit that grows on full-sized trees. Often people think they need to be all grown up or to look a certain way to see fruit of the Spirit grow. But God grows the same full-sized fruit in all people, no matter how old they are, no matter what they look like, where they've been, or what they've done. Granted, fruit doesn't grow overnight! It still takes many years of loving and following Christ for fruit to reach maturity, but God grows it the same in each of us regardless of our circumstances or appearance.

words or draw pictures of ways they show their assigned qualities to others. For example, if a student has "joy" written at the top of his or her cutout, the student could write or draw about encouraging someone who is sad by telling that person about Jesus, or by drawing that person jumping for joy or singing praise songs. When kids have finished, have them attach their completed cutouts to the smaller child's outline.

Say: **Wow! You all have so many awesome ways that you show others the fruit of God is growing in each of you! One way the fruit of the Spirit grows in our lives is when we see it growing in the lives of others—then we know what it's supposed to look like and how we should behave. And when other people see those gifts growing in your lives, you're showing them how God wants us to behave. God sent his Son, Jesus, to show us what our fruit should look like when it's fully grown. When we read our Bibles, we can see the perfect example of what our fruit should look like and how we should live for God.**

Encourage children to read the quality written at the top of their fruit cutouts. Have older children assist younger children with reading. Then have the kids write words or draw pictures that show how Jesus might have shown the assigned quality of the fruit of the Spirit. For example, if the quality listed is "love," children could show Jesus hugging a child or could write about his death on the cross. When they've finished, have each child come up to the Jesus outline and attach his or her fruit cutout inside the outline.

Say: **Those are all great things we can learn about the fruit of the Spirit by looking at Jesus! Remember, God sent Jesus to this earth to teach us how to live and to show us how to please God, right? So that means that the more we learn how to follow Jesus' example—the more we get to know about him, the more we learn to love him, and the more we try to be like him—the more God's love becomes part of us!**

Open your Bible to Galatians 5:22-23a, and say: **The apostle Paul tells us in Galatians, "But the fruit of the Spirit is love, joy, peace, patience, kindness, goodness, faithfulness, gentleness and self-control." Love, joy, peace, patience, kindness, goodness, faithfulness, gentleness, and self-control—these all describe God's love. And as we've just learned, the closer we become with Jesus every day, the more God's love becomes part of us. And God's love shows itself in us through...what is it called?** Allow children to respond. Say: **The fruit of the Spirit! The fruit of the Spirit *grows* in us, just as fruit that we eat grows on trees!**

Use a green marker to draw a rough outline of a treetop at the top of the

TOUR GUIDE TIP

Be sure to walk around and give suggestions for ways Jesus modeled each quality of the fruit of the Spirit, especially for younger children who are still learning who Jesus is and what he did. Some examples include: *love*—his death on the cross, how he talked with sinners and loved them, how he loved children; *joy*—how he rejoiced in knowing God has good plans and there is a better place to come, how he encouraged others to be happy not sad; *peace*—how he spent time in prayer to experience God's peace; *patience*—how he showed love even when people didn't listen to his words; *kindness*—how he was kind to everyone, not just popular people; *goodness*—how he made right choices and helped and healed others; *faithfulness*—how he was a loyal friend, especially to his disciples; *gentleness*—how he was loving and gentle in his words and actions; and *self-control*—how even though people mocked him or tried to hurt him, he kept his cool, knowing God was in control.

smaller child's outline. Turn the outline of the student into a tree, using the child's body as the tree trunk and his or her outstretched arms as the branches. Then have each child carefully remove the fruit they've just placed on the Jesus outline and place it at the top of the "tree," in the branches of the smaller child's outline.

Say: **The fruit of the Spirit grows in us. Say that with me!** Lead children in repeating the phrase. Say: **Now we can see by looking at our two outlines how those parts of Jesus—God's love—become part of us the closer we become with him. But why? Why would God want us to have parts of Jesus inside of us?** (Allow children to respond.) **Those are all good answers, but the main reason is that** 🕐 **God gives us the fruit of the Spirit to help us show others what his love looks like.**

Choose a child to read aloud John 15:4-5.

Have kids form pairs or trios to discuss the following questions:

• **What do you think Jesus means when he says to "remain in me"?**

• **What kind of fruit do you think Jesus is talking about? Have you seen those kinds of fruit in your lives? When?**

• **Why can't we grow the fruit by ourselves? Why do we want the fruit Jesus talks about?**

Say: **Our purpose here on earth is to love God and to show God's love to others.** 🕐 **God gives us the fruit of the Spirit to help us show others what his love looks like. The fruit of the Spirit is made up of various gifts that help us do a good job for our Father. Let's find out what each gift does!**

STORY EXCURSION (20 minutes)
Recipe for Success

Before this session, set up nine stations, each in a different room or a different area of your classroom. Stations can be as simple as a folding chair set up in nine different areas. At each station, have a sign that indicates which fruit of the Spirit quality will be highlighted. For the corresponding stations, provide a bowl of the following fruit: *love,* strawberries; *joy,* orange slices; *peace,* grapes; *patience,* banana slices; *kindness,* diced pears; *goodness,* apple slices; *faithfulness,* starfruit slices; *gentleness,* kiwi slices; *self-control,* maraschino cherries and nondairy whipped topping.

Turn your back to the children as you place a chef's hat on your head and put on an apron. Wheel around on your heel, sporting your best attempt at a French accent, and say: **Bonjour, mes amies! That means, as you folks say, "Hello, friends!" My name es Chef Tellzeetruth, zee world famous cree-a-tor of what I like to call... "fruit of zee Spirit salad"!** (Bow dramatically.) **Today,**

Items to Pack: nine large bowls with serving spoons, strawberries, orange slices, grapes, banana slices, diced pears, apple slices, starfruit slices, kiwi slices, maraschino cherries, nondairy whipped topping, paper and markers, paper bowls, chef's hat, apron, plastic forks, CD player, CD of soft music, CD of chaotic-sounding music

each one of you has been chosen as a special guest to learn my secret rec-i-pay. Come! Let us learn zee recipe for success!

Hand out paper or plastic foam bowls and forks to the students. Lead them to the station labeled "love."

Say: **Vehry well, now. Zis is zee very first an-gree-dee-ont in zee fruit of zee Spirit salad:** *Love.* **Ah, yes...zee love.** (Stare off dreamily; then suddenly snap out of it.) **Repeat after me: "Zee fruit of zee Spirit is love!" I use zee straw-berr-ees to represent love because zay are red, like a heart...or a big fat kiss! Find two people in zis room right now, and tell each person what you love about him or her!** Allow children a minute or two to do this.

Ask: • **What are zome of zee ways** *you* **show love to oth-eres?**

Say: **Tres bien, tres bien! Zat means "Very good! Very good!" Repeat after me: Zee fruit of zee Spirit is love!** (Have children respond.) **Now each of you put one straw-berr-ee in your bowl, and we will go get our next an-gree-dee-ont. Find a partner to hug as you walk!**

Lead children to the station labeled "joy."

Say: **Oh, what a happy little fruit we have here! Our next an-gree-dee-ont in zee fruit of zee Spirit salad is** *joy.* **Let's review zee an-gree-dee-onts in our salad so far. Zee fruit of zee Spirit is...what was at our last station? Love! And now we have...joy! Repeat after me: Zee fruit of zee Spirit is love and joy.** (Have children respond.) **Tres bien, tres bien!**

Now to represent joy in our salad, I like to use zee or-onge slice-es. Do you know why? (Allow children to guess.) **It's because zee or-onge slice-es look like little smiles when you put them in your mouths, like zis!** (Place an orange slice in your mouth to look like an orange smile.) **Now you try! Put an or-onge slice in your mouth, and find three people to smile at!** (Allow children a minute to do this.) **Bon! Now let's put them back in our bowls. Joy is all about smiles and the happiness zat only God can give.**

Ask: • **What are some ways you can share God's joy with others?**

Say: **Tres bien! Tres bien! Now repeat once more with me: Zee fruit of zee Spirit is what?** (Lead children in responding, "love and joy.") **Good! Now make sure you have an or-onge slice in your bowl, and let's move on! Think of a happy word to cheer us as we travel!**

Lead cheering children to the station labeled "peace."

Say: **Are you ready for zee next an-gree-dee-ont? It is** *peace!* **So now what an-gree-dee-onts do we have in zee fruit of zee Spirit salad?** (Lead children in saying, "Zee fruit of zee Spirit is love, joy, and peace!") **Very good! And to represent zee** *peace* **in our salad, I choose zee grape. I choose it because many of you have**

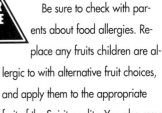

Be sure to check with parents about food allergies. Replace any fruits children are allergic to with alternative fruit choices, and apply them to the appropriate fruit of the Spirit quality. You also may choose to make fruit substitutions depending on the fruits that are in season at the time of this activity.

Strawberries were first cultivated in ancient Rome and used as a medicinal herb in the thirteenth century. How appropriate that we chose strawberries to represent love, because love is the best medicine for any hurt, sickness, or wound! Strawberries are also a member of the rose family, and everyone knows what the red rose symbolizes! So eat up!

SCENIC ROUTE →

Because of time constraints or space limitations, you may want to do a simplified version of this activity. Simply give each child a paper bowl, and instead of having kids travel to different stations, provide a large bowl of either mixed fruit or fruit-shaped candies or cereals. Use the dialogue as a rough outline, and have kids use their imaginations to pretend that they're receiving the specific fruits you talk about. Give each child a spoonful of fruit or a piece of candy or cereal for each fruit of the Spirit quality in this activity. Be sure to lead children in the actions and to discuss the questions for each quality.

probably heard zee term "world peace," yes? And zee grape is round like zee world, so it will help you remember zis fruit of zee Spirit salad an-gree-dee-ont. Find someone to give a grape to and say, "Peace, man!" Allow children to serve one another grapes.

Say: However, when people talk about world peace, zay usually are talking about people not fighting around the world. No wars. Zee peace God gives is diff-er-ont! It is a peace that helps us stop fighting with ourselves and with others—zee battles that happen in our hearts and in our heads. Think about zay time you've been afraid of something. Turn to a partner and zhare your stories.

Allow children time to share with one another. Then continue.

Say: God doesn't want us to worry about anything. He wants us to talk to him about our fears, about our problems, about everything. God will take care of our battles for us so that we can have his perfect peace. So...a-noth-ere fruit of zee Spirit is *peace*. Instruct children to freeze and remain still for a minute as you play some soft music. You may want to turn off the lights or instruct children to close their eyes. Explain that this is what peace feels like inside.

Ask: • When have you felt God's peace inside?

Say: Let's review our an-gree-dee-onts once more. Repeat after me: Zee fruit of zee Spirit is love, joy, and peace. (Allow children to respond.) Tres bien! Tres bien! Now I'll reveal zee next secret an-gree-dee-ont! Everyone walk *quietly* and in peace over here.

Lead kids quietly to the station labeled "patience."

Say: Tah-dah! Zee next part of our fruit of zee Spirit salad! I bet you are all getting hungry aren't you? That's why we add zee next fruit: *patience*.

Now we *could* eat our salad as it is...a strawberry, an orange, maybe even zee grape. But...if we waited until we have all of zee proper an-gree-dee-onts...ooh la la! We need to add zis patience. Have kids form a line and wait their turns to get their pieces of fruit.

Say: I choose zee banana to represent zee patience because how many of you have ever had your parents bring home bananas from zee gro-cer-ee store that were bright, bright *green*? (Allow children to respond.) Ah ha, yes, I see! And do green bananas taste very good? Not really. So what did you have to do? (Allow children to respond.) Zat's right! You had to wait for zee bananas to ripen. And zen, zee bananas turn *wonderful*! You all had to wait your turn to get your fruit, and now...wonderful! Tres bien! Tres bien! So repeat after me: Zee fruit of zee Spirit is love, joy, peace, and *patience*. (Allow children to respond.) Very good.

Ask: • When have you had to be patient about something that turned out mag-nee-fee-cant but took a *long* time?

Say: **God gives us patience to help us know that he always has what is best planned for us—it just might take a little bit of time before we get it. And we know that God is patient with us! Even when we goof up and disobey God, God waits for us to make the right choices and follow him again. God loves us even when we're not showing love to him. So** *patience* **is another part of the fruit of zee Spirit.**

What are zee other an-gree-dee-onts to our fruit of zee Spirit salad? (Lead kids in responding, "Love, joy, peace, and patience.") **Bon! That means "good!" Now let's move on.**

Lead children to the station labeled "kindness." Say: **Our next an-gree-dee-ont es zee** *kindness*! **Zat is correct. I choose zee pear to represent kindness because I have a pear tree in my back yard in Paris. Oui, oui! Zat pear tree, every year, without fail, she gives and gives and gives, so many delicious pears to help me cook zee grand masterpieces zat make me zee world-famous Chef Tellzeetruth. And when I think of kindness, I think of God's kindness— how he gives and helps me and always wants zee best for me every single day. Find a person beside you to show kindness to right now by carrying his or her bowl to the next station.**

So now what are our an-gree-dee-onts to our fruit of zee Spirit salad? Zee fruit of zee Spirit is [have kids fill in "love, joy, peace, patience, and kindness"]. **Tres bien! Tres bien!**

Ask: • **How has God shown kindness to you?**

Allow children to respond.

Say: **Wonderful! Wonderful! Put a scoop of pears in your friend's bowl to show kindness to your friend and to remember God's kindness to us. But before we go, remind me of zee fruit of zee Spirit once more!** Lead kids in saying, "Zee fruit of zee Spirit is love, joy, peace, patience, and kindness."

Lead children to the next station, labeled "goodness."

Say: **Our fruit of zee Spirit salads are almost zere! Our next an-gree-dee-ont es zee** *goodness*. **As in, "Oh, my goodness, what a salad!" I choose zee app-le to represent zee goodness because...well...it is just so good! And zat is what God wants our lives to be filled with—goodness. So, tell me zee an-gree-dee-onts all together! Zee fruit of zee Spirit is** [lead children in filling in "love, joy, peace, patience, kindness, and goodness"]. **Put a good apple slice in your friend's bowl, and then give the bowl back to him or her.**

Ask: • **How has God been good to you? How can you show God's goodness to others?**

Say: C'est magnifique! It's magnificent! One more time! Zee fruit of zee **Spirit is** [lead children in filling in "love, joy, peace, patience, kindness, and goodness"]. **On we go!**

Lead children to the next station labeled "faithfulness."

Say: **Welcome, mes amies, to zee an-gree-dee-ont zat no one else knows about in my salads. Look at zee fruit! It is zee starfruit! And do you know why? Because many, many years before Jesus was born, God promised through his prophets to send his Son, the Messiah. And one day, he did! Zere was a bright and mag-nee-fee-cant star in zee sky, and it led zee wise men to find baby Jesus. Zat star—it reminds us of God's *faithfulness*. And faithfulness is our next an-gree-dee-ont.**

Faithfulness means zat God is true to his promises. It means he is loyal and is always with us. It means we can trust zat every word in zee Bible is true.

Ask: • When have you seen God be faithful to you or your family? How can you be faithful to someone?

Say: **Before we leave—quick! What is zee fruit of zee Spirit?** (Lead children in responding, "love, joy, peace, patience, kindness, goodness, and faithfulness.")

Good! Now place a star in your bowl, just as God placed zee star in zee sky over Bethlehem. Stir up your salads, my friends, and let us away to zee next station. Link arms with a partner to walk to our next station, so you can remember how God sticks with us because he's faithful, and how we should stick to our friends.

Lead children to the station labeled, "gentleness."

Say: ***Gentleness* is zee next an-gree-dee-ont. I choose zee kiwi fruit to represent zee gentleness. And do you know why? It is because—well, look at zis thing!** (Hold up an uncut kiwi fruit.) **It is uggg—ly! Zis fruit looks like Mr. Toughguy on zee outside, doesn't he? But look inside, my friends.** (Slice the kiwi open.) **He is just a big Mr. Mushball on zee insides! Don't get me wrong—I wouldn't want to mess with him! All that tough skin and spiky hair—I am afraid of zee kiwi fruit! But I know zat he is soft and sweet on zee inside—and zat is why I also love zee kiwi fruit.**

God is gentle—just like zee kiwi. We should respect God—because we know he is more powerful and tougher than *anything*! But we should also love God, because we know God is love and wants to bless us. Let's discover zee diff-er-ohnce right now by turning to a partner and saying in a gentle voice, "Please be nice to mes amies." That means, "Please be nice to my friends." (Allow children to respond.) **Bon. Now turn to your partner and say, "Please be nice to mes amies!" in a *not* gentle voice.** (Allow children to respond.) **Which**

way of speaking do you think is better? Which would you be more willing to listen to if someone said it to you?

So our new an-gree-dee-ont is zee gentleness. Say it with me now: Zee fruit of zee Spirit is [lead children in filling in "love, joy, peace, patience, kindness, goodness, faithfulness, and gentleness"].

Tres bien!

Ask: • When have you seen God's gentleness in your life? How could you show it to someone else?

Say: Bon! Now place zee gentle kiwi fruit in zee salad, and let us move on to zee grand finale in our masterpieces!

Lead children to the station labeled "self-control."

Say: Voila! Zee grand finale in our fruit of zee Spirit salads! It is zee *self-control*. Say it with me, friends—self-control. And do you know why zee last an-gree-dee-ont es zee self-control? It is because it is my favorite! Zee whipped cream and zee cherry on top! We must have self-control with zis an-gree-dee-ont or we get zee big belly! Zen I must get zee new apron. Whisper: One size does not fit all.

Say: Anyhoo—zis is it: self-control. God wants us to have self-control so that we behave as Christ and make choices about our words and actions that are pleasing to God. What would happen if we did not have zee self-control? What would our world look like? Instruct children to set down their bowls and move away from the food. Play some music that sounds chaotic or very fast, and have kids move wildly for ten seconds to express what *no* self-control looks like. When you turn off the music, have kids freeze and wait for you to ask the discussion questions.

Say: Wow! How crazy would that be to have zee people running around everywhere, only worrying about zemselves instead of oth-eres?

Ask: • Why do we need to have self-control in our lives?

• When have you had to have self-control with something?

Say: Very good! Now take a look at your salads. Add zee final an-gree-dee-onts.

Tell me now, what is zee fruit of zee Spirit? (Lead children in shouting, "Love, joy, peace, patience, kindness, goodness, faithfulness, gentleness, and self-control!") Remember to have self-control as you enjoy zee fruit of zee Spirit salad! Bon appe-teet!

Allow children time to sit and eat their fruit salads before moving on to the next activity.

Items to Pack: prism, light source, props (optional)

SCENIC ROUTE → You may want to have kids perform their commercials completely in mime, to remind them of how our actions should speak loudly to others.

SCENIC ROUTE → Have kids perform their commercials in front of a video recorder. Afterward, allow them to watch their taped commercials. You may even want to show the commercials to the rest of the congregation at your church to show the cool things the kids at your church are doing. This is also a great way to recruit volunteers!

ADVENTURES IN GROWING

(15 minutes)
Lemme See!

Set a prism in an area where the direct sunlight shines through it to make a rainbow, or use a flashlight to create the effect.

Say: God gives us the fruit of the Spirit to help us show others what his love looks like. A way to help us remember that is to look at this prism. God is like the light—he is pure, and he shines into our lives with his love, joy, peace, patience, kindness, goodness, faithfulness, gentleness, and self-control. All of those traits were in Jesus. And when Jesus was on earth, he told us that each one of us—no matter how old or how young, how little or big—has a job to do! That job is to tell others about God's love for them. One of the loudest ways we can tell someone about God's love is by *showing* it to that person.

Look at that rainbow created by the light through the prism. We are like the prism. When we know Jesus and accept God's love, it shines beautifully through us. That rainbow doesn't have to make a noise to speak to us, does it?

Have kids work in groups of four or five, including older and younger kids on the same teams. Assign each group a fruit of the Spirit quality, and give kids several minutes to think of a way they could create a commercial for their assigned character trait. Allow kids to be creative and to use or create props if they would like. Ask them to imagine that they're trying to sell their fruit of the Spirit to someone who has never heard of it. Encourage them to think about why their fruit of the Spirit is important, what it does for people, why people need it, and what they think is great about their fruit of the Spirit. You may want to move around to each group to assist kids with ideas. When kids have had time to practice, have each group perform its commercial for everyone. Be sure to applaud every group's efforts. The following is an example of a simple commercial:

Ben: *(Approaching a girl who is sitting alone and crying)* Excuse me, miss. What seems to be the problem?

Angie: *(Looking up sadly)* My dog ran away, I didn't make the soccer team, and my best friend is moving away! That's what the problem is! Boohoo!

Ben: *(Pulling out a bottle of Joy liquid soap or a piece of fruit)* I think what you need is *joy*! That's right, joy, the fruit of the Spirit!

Angie: How's joy going to help me? I feel miserable!

Ben: *(Motions to boy offstage)* Come tell us about it, Steve! *(Steve enters.)* With joy your face will be smiling! *(Steve smiles widely.)* You'll be jumping up and down because you're happy God loves you! *(Steve jumps up and down.)* You may even be able to laugh when bad things happen because you know that God is bigger than all your problems! *(Steve laughs hysterically, shrugging his shoulders.)*

Angie: Well...how much does it cost?

Ben: That's the best part! It's absolutely free! All you have to do is follow Jesus' example and love God. Oh, yeah...I should warn you...it's contagious.

(Steve walks over to another girl sitting nearby and crying. He smiles at her, jumps for joy, and begins laughing while shrugging his shoulders and looking up. He puts his arm around the girl. The girl smiles, begins jumping for joy, and the two skip off, laughing hysterically.)

For students who are shy or who may not be into the drama scene, you may choose to provide an option of working together to draw a picture that shows what their fruit of the Spirit quality does and why we need it. Have students then describe their pictures.

SOUVENIRS (15 minutes)
Fruit Suit

Using fruit-shaped candies, markers, and glue, the children will make their very own fruit mosaic suits to remind them of what the fruits on their insides must show to the rest of the world. These mosaics will become the first page of their Travel Journals.

Items to Pack: for each child, one copy of the "Fruit Suit" handout (p. 19), fruit-shaped candies, markers, glue, glue brushes, small dishes

Say: 🌀 **God gives us fruit of the Spirit to help us show others what his love looks like. God's love is Jesus, his one and only Son, who he gave to each of us on the cross. Jesus paid the price for our sins so that we could be with God in heaven forever. When we accept God's gift of Jesus, that love is inside of us. It's there in the form of love, joy, peace, patience, kindness, goodness, faithfulness, gentleness, and self-control.**

We can't ever pay God back for his love for us. But we can obey his commands to love him and to love our neighbors. God wants us to show everyone we meet what his love looks like. But how will they know what God's love looks like if we don't show them? What if we just keep it all inside? Is it doing any good for God or for anyone else? No way! If you could wear God's love on the outside, what would it look like?

Give each student a photocopy of the "Fruit Suit" handout (p. 19). Set out several bowls of fruit-shaped candies, some glue brushes, and dishes of glue. Instruct children to design a suit they could wear that would show others what God's love looks like. Demonstrate how to spread glue on their pages with the glue brushes and then place the colored candy fruits in designs that symbolize fruit of the Spirit to them. For example, they may use the red candies to make heart shapes on the outfit, symbolizing love. They could simply make a multicolored design to show the many colors of God's love to others, which they learned about from the prism demonstration. Allow kids to be creative, and encourage them to really think about what features they add to their suits.

When students have finished, ask:

• **What does your suit tell others about God's love?**

• **What other ways could you show God's love?**

• **Why do you think God doesn't give us a suit to wear to show his love to others? Why does he grow his love inside of us?**

Items to Pack: Bible, bowl of grapes

HOME AGAIN PRAYER

(5 minutes)

Have kids sit down. Open your Bible once again and read John 15:4-5. Pass around a bowl of grapes as you lead children in the following prayer. When the bowl comes to each child, have that child say a fruit of the Spirit gift he or she would like God's help to show others and then eat a grape.

Pray: **Heavenly Father, we love you and thank you for the gifts of the fruit of the Spirit. Thank you for giving us what we need to show others your love. We know that Jesus is the vine and we are the branches and that without Jesus, we can't show anyone your love. We thank you for Jesus, and as we eat this fruit, may your fruit grow within us so that it shines to all those around us. Please help us to show every day your** [Have children fill in their desired fruit of the Spirit gift]. **Thank you, Father. In Jesus' name, amen.**

Fruit Suit

Love

Pathway Point: 🌑 God wants us to love as he does.

In-Focus Verse: "God is love. Whoever lives in love lives in God, and God in him" (1 John 4:16b).

Travel Itinerary

Elementary-aged children are eager to accept the love of God because of their childlike faith. But knowing what God's love looks like is a different story. Kids are familiar with the feeling of love, and they enjoy showing their own love to others, through hugs and kisses, cleaning a bedroom without being asked, or making a homemade card. During this journey kids will learn about love as a choice and as an action that shows others what God looks like, rather than as a feeling. They will discover that God is love and that he sent his Son, Jesus, to earth to model love in action. The more children learn to live as Christ demonstrated, the more they can share God's love with others. They'll learn why God wants us to love one another: so that his love will be complete. And they'll learn how the Bible tells us to show love to one another as the fruit of the Spirit grows within us.

Items to Pack: yarn, a bowl of beads or looped cereal

DEPARTURE PRAYER

(5 minutes)

Children pray regularly for the people they love—moms, dads, grandmas, and grandpas. Praying for others is definitely a sign of God's love. Bring this to the attention of your students. Explain to kids that God is love and when God is in our lives, love is in our lives and must be shared through our actions. Have kids pass around a piece of yarn, knotted at one end. Place a bowl of beads or looped cereal pieces in the middle of your circle. Encourage each child to think of several people to pray for. For each person a child thinks of (try to limit each child to no more than five people), have the child choose that many beads and, during the appropriate time in the prayer, place the beads on the necklace when it comes around.

Pray: **God, we love you so much. We love you because you first loved us, and we know that you are love. Please help us be like Jesus and share with others the love you put in us, so they can see you. Help us show your love to others—even to those who don't show love to us. Right now we pray for these special people in our lives: [Have kids pass around the knotted string, add** their beads, and say the names of the people in their lives who the beads represent]. **Help us always to choose love and to be more like Jesus each day. In Jesus' name, amen.**

1st STOP DISCOVERY (15 minutes)
Mirror, Mirror

This activity helps kids discover that the love we show others is a reflection of God's love in us.

Items to Pack: Bible

Help children form pairs. Say: **What do you think of when you hear the word "love"?** (Allow children to respond.) **A lot of times, we think of love as a feeling—like we** *love* **ice cream, or we just** *love* **it when our birthday comes. Although those feelings are good, it's important to understand that God's love is different. God's love is always there. Let's see what the Bible tells us love is.** Open your Bible, and have a volunteer read aloud 1 Corinthians 13:4-7.

Say: **Wow! The Bible tells us that love is a lot of things! But one of the most important things to remember is found in 1 John 4:16.** Choose a different volunteer to read aloud 1 John 4:16. Say: **The Bible tells us that God** *is* **love! So that means when we have God in our lives, we have love in our lives. As we grow in God, love will grow in us!** 🌀 **God wants us to love as he does—to show others what he is all about.**

Have children form pairs. Say: **Let me show you what I mean. Choose one person in your pair to be the "leader" and the other to be the "follower." I'm going to give you a situation. The leader should act out a response that shows God's love. I'd like the follower to do exactly what the leader does—so you look like a mirror image of the leader.**

Read the first of the following situations, and have the leaders create actions for the followers to imitate. After acting out a situation, partners will change roles and then act out the next situation.

Situation 1: You are trying to leave the house to get to your soccer tournament. You put all your equipment on and are ready to go—but your little brother is making you late because he can't yet tie his shoes. Act out how you could show love by being patient and helpful.

2. You sit at a table eating lunch with all your friends at school. Your friends start pointing to the end of the table where a new kid sits alone. Your friends start laughing. Act out how you could show love by being kind to the new kid.

3. Your dad has just returned from work and says that he's had a really bad

day. He looks as if he needs to just relax, but he has to take out the trash first. Act out how you could show love to your dad.

4. You've saved your money for a long time to buy the new scooter you've always wanted. You've just bought the scooter, but your little brother really wants to try it out. You know that he's too little to play on the scooter and he might wreck it or hurt himself. Act out how you could show love to your little brother.

Have children discuss the following questions with their partners and then share their answers with the whole group.

Ask: • Why is doing the loving thing sometimes hard?

• Why is it always best to do the loving thing?

• What was it like to try to mirror or follow the leader?

• How can we mirror or follow God's example of loving others?

Say: Sometimes it's hard to love others. We need to remember that God loves us all the time—even when we don't deserve it. Let's mirror God's example and love as he does.

STORY EXCURSION (15 minutes)
Love Connection

Give each child a white or light-colored balloon. Set out colored markers for kids to share.

Open your Bible to 1 John 4:8, and choose a child to read the verse aloud. Say: **Wow! Love is a *choice* we make to show others what God's all about. Our verse just told us that if we choose *not* to love, we're telling the world that we don't know God. Because what did the Bible say God is?** (Allow children to respond.) **God is love. Everyone, say that with me.** (Lead children in repeating, "God is love.") **Cool!**

It's important for us to learn there are many things we can do or say to show God's love to others. 🕐 **God wants us to love as he does. But if we don't have that love inside us, our actions and words don't mean anything to God. For example, we could go to a homeless shelter and serve people food. If we do it with love, with a joyful attitude and a listening ear, people are going to see what God looks like! They're going to see love! But if we go to a homeless shelter and serve food while we're all angry about being there, rude and complaining, we've only done an action. It didn't show love. We've told the world that we don't know God. God's love can be shown to others only through *us*! Isn't that cool?**

Right now I want you to draw a picture on your flattened balloon. I want you to think about one way you can choose to love someone, or to show God's love to others, and draw it on the balloon.

When children have finished their drawings, have them form four groups. Have each group stand single file on one side of the room. Say: **When you come up with a way to show God's love to others, as you just did in your drawings, it's important to ask God to help you do it. Without God inside us—without his love—our actions don't really mean anything.**

Inflate a balloon. Say: **We're kind of like these balloons—we can't really do much on our own. But God's love is like the air in this balloon. It fills us and gives us power.** (Release the balloon and let it fly around the room.) **With God's love in me, I can do all kinds of things for him! Let's play a game in which you get to try this.**

Instruct children to pick up their balloons and straighten their lines. Tell the first child in each line to inflate his or her balloon as fast as possible and then release it toward the finish line, on the other side of the room. The next players in line will watch where the first person's balloon lands, run to the balloon, throw it back to the person who just let it go, inflate his or her own balloon, and release it toward the finish line.

In their groups, have kids answer the following questions:

Ask: • **How far would the balloons have gone if you'd let them go without inflating them first?**

• **How is the air in the balloon like God's love?**

• **How has God helped you show love to someone else?**

• **How else can you show God's love to others?**

SCENIC ROUTE → When children have finished the game, have them inflate and tie off their balloons. Give each child a long piece of chenille wire, and help children wrap one end around the tied-off part of the balloon. Be sure each child's name is on his or her balloon; then collect all the balloons into a large bouquet. Display the bouquet somewhere in your room or your church to show what the kids are learning.

ADVENTURES IN GROWING

(10 to 15 minutes)
Solid Love

This activity helps kids discover how they can make choices to love every day, growing closer to God and becoming more like Jesus.

Items to Pack: Bible, three large sheets of paper, marker, masking tape

Before children arrive, tape up large sheets of paper in three corners or areas of your room. Designate one corner to represent answers that show love to God, and write the word "God" on the taped piece of paper. In another corner, write the word "others," and have that corner represent answers that show love to others. In the third corner of the room, write the words, "no one" on the sheet of paper, and have that corner represent answers that show no love.

Say: **In John 14:15 Jesus tells us, "If you love me, you will obey what I command." And in John 15:17 Jesus tells us, "This is my command: Love each other."** This may sound like a pretty easy command when you think of people you really like—your mom, your dad, grandmas, grandpas, brothers, sisters, aunts, uncles, and friends. But God wants us to love *everyone*—the kid that picks on you at school, the kid that nobody talks to at school because she's "different," *everyone*! That's a difficult thing to do sometimes! But Jesus didn't hang out with the cool kids. He hung out with people who nobody liked. Jesus showed love to everyone, and he helps us love everyone too. We have the fruit of the Spirit quality of love to use as our secret weapon! ◐ God wants us to love as he does. And God *gives* love to us as we grow closer to him.

Explain to kids that you will read some everyday situations they may encounter. Have all the kids stand in the middle of the room. Tell them to listen to each situation and think about whether love is being shown to God, to others, or to no one at all. When you have finished reading the scenario, shout "Go!" and have the kids run to the corner that they think best represents to whom love is being shown.

Say: **Here's the first situation: Your entire class is going on a field trip to a Buddhist temple. While on the field trip, students will learn how to do some of the Buddhist practices and learn how to chant. You decide that you don't want to go on this field trip and stay behind at the school with a teacher. Who does this show love to?** Go! When children have run to their chosen corners, read aloud Exodus 20:3.

Say: **A friend at school just received the new CD you've been wanting for a long time. You decide to take it from your friend's locker and "borrow" it for a little while. Who does this show love to?** Go! When children have run to their chosen corners, read aloud Exodus 20:15.

Say: **Your friend at school had his favorite CD stolen from his locker. You have the very same CD at home and know that your friend likes it way better than you do. You decide to give your friend the CD as a replacement. Who does this show love to?** Go! When children have run to their chosen corners, read aloud Romans 12:13.

Say: **A girl in your neighborhood has been telling lies about your friend to the rest of the kids on your block. Now nobody wants to play with your friend. You decide to stand up to the girl and tell her she's not being nice. Who are you showing love to?** Go! When children have run to their chosen corners, read aloud Romans 12:10.

Say: **A friend of yours brings over a movie that you know your parents don't want you to see. You explain to your friend that you have to obey your**

TOUR GUIDE TIP

Children may have different responses to each situation, and that's OK! Some situations may have more than one answer. If children go to different corners, ask children in each corner to share why they chose the answers they did.

FUN FACT

In 270 A.D., Bishop Valentine secretly performed marriage ceremonies against the demands of Claudius II, the Roman emperor. The emperor did not want men to get married during times of war because he felt married men made poor soldiers. Bishop Valentine was jailed and executed on February 14, which is why people now celebrate Valentine's Day on that date.

parents. Instead of playing your friend's movie, you decide to put in a movie you've both seen a hundred times. The two of you have a contest to see who can recite the most lines! Who does this show love to? Go! When children have run to their chosen corners, read aloud Exodus 20:12.

Say: You get a new street bike for your birthday. All day long at school, you can think only about riding your bike, learning new tricks on your bike, and ways to make your bike even cooler. Every spare moment you get, you polish your bike, wash the tires, and add stickers to it. If your little brother even *thinks* about touching your bike, you will make him pay for it. Who does this show love to? Go! When children have run to their chosen corners, read aloud Hebrews 13:16.

Say: All your friends have decided to cheat on the spelling test at school. Your best friend passes around the answers to anyone who wants them. You tell your friend, "No thanks. I stayed up way too late studying for this thing!" Who does this show love to? Go! When children have run to their chosen corners, read aloud Leviticus 19:11.

Say: You and your best friend love to pick on his little brother. One day you take the little brother's bike and hide it from him. As you ride away laughing, you hit a stone in the street and flip off your own bike. Your friend's little brother races over to help you up and then runs to get an adult to help you. Who does this show love to? Go! When children have run to their chosen corners, read aloud 1 Corinthians 13:4-7.

Say: Every day each of us faces situations that allow us to make the choice to love. We have the Bible as our guidebook to help us know how to make the right choices. Remember, all we have to do is think about what Jesus would do. Jesus showed us how to love. He showed us how to love God and how to love others. And we can choose to love God and to love others by following Jesus' example.

SOUVENIRS (15 minutes)
Eternal Valentines

Using lace, markers, sequins, glitter glue, glue, and the "Eternal Valentine" handouts, children will make cross-shaped valentines to help them understand that we should tell others about God's love every day of the year.

Say: God showed us what true love looks like when he sent his Son, Jesus, to die on the cross for our sins. You see, God loves each one of us so

▲ **TOUR GUIDE TIP** This activity provides an excellent opportunity to present the gospel to children who haven't yet become Christians. If you sense a child might like to know more about what it means to follow Jesus, give this simple explanation: Say: **God loves us so much that he sent his Son, Jesus, to die on the cross for us. Jesus died and rose again so we could be forgiven for all the wrong things we do. Jesus wants to be our forever friend. If we ask him to, he'll take away the wrong things we've done and fill our lives with his love. As our forever friend, Jesus will always be with us and will help us make the right choices. And if we believe in Jesus, someday we'll live with him forever in heaven.**

You may also want to lead the child in a simple prayer, inviting Jesus to be his or her forever friend.

Share the news of the child's spiritual development with his or her parent(s) and celebrate!

Items to Pack: lace, markers, sequins, glitter glue, glue, photocopies of the "Eternal Valentine" handout (p. 27)

SCENIC ROUTE →

If time permits, have kids make more than one valentine. To make valentines more exciting, have kids use safety scissors to cut out their decorated crosses and then glue them to sheets of colored construction paper. Have kids punch holes in the construction paper and fasten the pages into their Travel Journals.

Items to Pack: Bible

much, and he wants every single one of us to be with him in heaven forever. The only way we can be there is to accept his gift of Jesus, who already paid the price for us to get into heaven. 1 John 4:19 tells us that we love because God first loved us. 🌑 God wants us to love as he does. We need to show and spread God's love every single day of the year!

So right now, we're going to create some not-so-ordinary valentines. I want you to use this lace, glitter, and sequins to make a valentine that tells someone about the true love of Jesus. Use your markers to write or draw pictures of whatever you would want to tell someone about God's love!

When children have finished, have them present their valentines to the class and explain who they will give them to.

HOME AGAIN PRAYER (5 minutes)

Have kids sit down. Open your Bible and read 1 John 4:15-16. Lead children in the following prayer. When you come to the words, "We will share the love that you give us," have children stand up and hug the people on either side of them, and then continue the prayer.

Pray: **God, we love you and thank you for the fruit of the Spirit you give us in love. Thank you for loving us first to show us what true love looks like. We thank you for the gift of Jesus and for helping us learn that we can always count on your love that grows inside us. We thank you for teaching us how to love because you are love. We will share the love that you give us.** (Have children stand and hug.) **We praise you and love you because you are God and you are love. In Jesus' name, amen.**

Eternal Valentine

Joy

Pathway Point: Knowing Jesus gives us joy.

In-Focus Verse: "May the God of hope fill you with all joy and peace as you trust in him, so that you may overflow with hope by the power of the Holy Spirit" (Romans 15:13).

Travel Itinerary

Although children don't regularly use the word "joy," most children understand this word to mean "happiness." However, to a child, happiness often relates to something tangible, such as ice cream for dessert, a new toy from the store, or a visit from Grandma. This lesson helps teach children that "joy" means a permanent condition of the heart and an attitude that comes from having a personal relationship with Jesus. Through the workings of the Holy Spirit, we can have joy in our lives and be happy in good times and in difficult times. This lesson encourages children to express joy in the Lord at all times.

Items to Pack: red construction paper, markers, double-sided tape

DEPARTURE PRAYER (5 minutes)

Before praying, give each child a small piece of red construction paper. Have each child write the word "joy" on his or her paper with a marker. Place a strip of double-sided tape on the back of the paper. Have children repeat after you, line by line, the following prayer. As kids say the first line, encourage them to place the papers on their chests, like name tags.

Say: **Dear God,**

Fill my heart with joy (place tag on chest)

And give my face a smile. (Point to smiling mouth.)

Help me to be happy

For miles and miles and miles.

Amen.

SCENIC ROUTE → Purchase large heart stickers, and have kids use markers to write "joy" on the stickers. During the prayer, attach the stickers instead of the tags.

1st STOP DISCOVERY (15 minutes) **Filled With Joy**

The children will make take-home containers to fill with "happy" things.

Place all supplies on the table. Make sure to have one "fuel tank" container per person. Gather children around you on the floor.

28

Say: We're learning about the fruit of the Spirit. Last time, we learned about having love for God and others. Today we'll learn about another fruit of the Spirit quality. Let's get started!

Ask: • Before you leave for a long car trip, what are some of the things you and your parents do?

Allow children to answer the question.

Say: Before we take a long trip in our car, we must make sure we fill the tank with gas. Without gas in our car, we can't get very far. Listen to this verse from Psalm 126:3. Open your Bible and read the verse.

Ask: • What does it mean to be "filled with joy"?

Say: Sometimes we think the word "joy" means the same thing as the word "happiness." And, in some ways, the two words are a lot alike. We say we are happy when we get to play with our friends. Or we say we are happy when we get our favorite cookie for dessert. We're happy when we're watching our favorite television show.

Ask: • How do you feel when your favorite show is over?

• How do you feel when your favorite toy gets broken?

Say: Lots of things make us happy. But if something changes, as when our favorite toy breaks, then we may not be happy any longer. We can be really happy when Grandma comes to visit us, but it makes us sad for her to leave.

Joy means more than just being happy. The Bible tells us the fruit of the Spirit is love and joy. Joy is an attitude or a feeling that Jesus gives you when you have him in your heart. When Jesus is in your heart and you know you have a home forever with him in heaven, you have real joy. Your heart is full of joy. ◑ Knowing Jesus gives us joy. You may still be sad that a toy is broken or that you fell and hurt your knee, but that can't take away the joy you have by knowing Jesus. We can have joy during the good times, happy times, and fun times. But we can also have joy during the sad times, difficult times, or even scary times.

Remember the verse I read earlier, "The Lord has done great things for us, and we are filled with joy"? The verse reminds us that we can be happy and joyful because God has done so many wonderful things for us.

Ask: • What good thing has God done for you?

Say: God does so many wonderful, great things for us that we can't even count our blessings. Those blessings fill our hearts with joy.

I asked you earlier what you needed to do before taking a long car trip, and someone said that you'd need to fill the gas tank with fuel. Our verse says that *we* are filled with *joy*. Let's make a pretend gas tank. But we're going

Items to Pack: Bible, empty milk jugs or other plastic containers, red construction paper, scissors, markers, drawing paper, crayons, glue

TOUR GUIDE TIP

If you don't have enough plastic containers, have children cut two large hearts from red construction paper and glue together the sides and bottom of the heart, forming a basket. Add ribbon to make handles, and have the children hang the baskets in their rooms.

TOUR GUIDE TIP

Rather than drawing pictures, older children may prefer to write words on their slips of paper to describe events that make them happy.

Items to Pack: Bible, wading pool, sand, plastic measuring cups (one-half cup size), spoons

to let our pretend gas tanks be like our hearts. And instead of filling our "tanks" with gas, we're going to fill our tanks with joy.

Let each child choose a milk jug or plastic container. Encourage children to draw and cut hearts from red construction paper. Then have kids glue the hearts to the outside of their tanks. Give each child five small pieces of drawing paper, and encourage kids to draw five pictures of the ways God has blessed them. Encourage children to draw pictures of friends, family members, their homes, or favorite toys.

When children have finished drawing, form groups of three. Have each child explain his or her pictures. Then have kids stuff their pictures into their tanks. Encourage children to take home their pretend gas tanks. Invite them to add one or two pictures daily of something that happened that made them happy, keeping their tanks "filled with joy."

Say: **When you put these pictures in your pretend gas tank, remember there's a difference between being happy and having joy. Real joy means having Jesus in your heart and knowing that you will live forever with him in heaven.**

Ask: • **How does it make you feel to know that you will live with Jesus forever?** 🌑 Knowing Jesus gives us joy. Let's experience that joy now!

STORY EXCURSION (15 minutes)
Overflowing With Joy

To show that our hearts overflow with joy from God's blessings, children will use spoons to fill a measuring cup with sand until it overflows.

Before class, put sand in a wading pool or in a large, shallow container. Place measuring cups and spoons in the sand.

Open your Bible to Romans 15:13.

Say: **Listen to this verse from Romans: "May the God of hope fill you with all joy and peace as you trust in him, so that you may overflow with hope by the power of the Holy Spirit."**

Ask: • **What would happen if you left the water running in the bathtub and the plug was in?**

• **What does "overflow" mean?**

• **Can you tell me how you would feel if your heart were "overflowing with joy"?**

Say: **The Bible tells us that God will fill us with so much joy and happiness when we trust in him that we will overflow with hope. God fills our** hearts with such great joy when we believe in Jesus. Jesus just keeps filling our hearts with joy until we are "overflowing" with joy and happiness.

Let's play a fun game to remind us of the joy we have in our hearts.

Form groups of three. Have one child in each group hold a measuring cup over a wading pool or a large container of sand. On "Go," the other children in each team will quickly pour spoonfuls of sand into the cup. See how quickly each group can cause the cup to overflow.

Ask: • What happened to the sand when the cup could no longer hold it?

• If our hearts are full of joy and Jesus keeps blessing us with more joy, what do you think will happen?

• When you are happy and full of joy, how does that make the people around you feel?

Say: God blesses us with so many wonderful things, and he fills our hearts with joy. Even when our hearts are full of joy, he just keeps on giving us good things. In a way, our joy can overflow as our sand did and spill out. When our joy "spills," it can spill onto other people around us and make them happy, too. We can share our joy and happiness with those around us. ◑ Knowing Jesus gives us joy, and we can especially share our joy when we tell others about Jesus. We want others to know the joy of having Jesus in their hearts.

(10 minutes)
Joyful Jumble

Have children make this yummy, fun snack.

Say: When our hearts overflow with the joy Jesus gives us, we want to share that joy with others. Let's share a snack and talk about how we can share the joy of Jesus.

Let the children create their own snack mix from these ingredients: joyful jelly beans, happy Honey Nut Cheerios, rejoicing raisins, beaming banana chips, pleased pretzels, and glad grapes. Form groups of six (or the number of ingredients you decide to use). Give each member of the group a small bowl of one of the ingredients, a plastic spoon, and a small, resealable bag.

Have the first child complete this message: "Jesus gives me joy. I can share that joy by [examples: sharing my toys, smiling at others, hugging a friend, saying a kind word]." When the child completes the sentence, have that child place one scoop from his or her bowl into each child's plastic bag, including his or her own.

TOUR GUIDE TIP You could use water for this activity if you don't have access to sand.

SCENIC ROUTE → For extra impact, bring in a microscope and let children look at a small amount of sand. Point out how small the grains are and that a spoonful of sand holds many, many grains of sand. Explain how Jesus blesses our lives with so many wonderful things, both big and little.

Items to Pack: jelly beans; Honey Nut Cheerios; raisins; banana chips; pretzels; grapes; plastic bowls; plastic spoons; small, resealable plastic bags

TOUR GUIDE TIP It's always a good idea to check with parents about allergies before giving snacks to the children in your class. You can use any snack items that work for your group rather than the ones suggested in this activity.

Items to Pack: Bible, masking tape

After each child has had a turn, read 1 Thessalonians 5:16: "Be joyful always." Have children repeat the verse after you. Give thanks for the good snack, ask God to help you share Jesus' joy with others, and then eat!

(10 to 15 minutes)
Always Rejoice

Children will learn from this game that we can have joy in our hearts during good times and bad times.

Use masking tape to make a finish line on the floor.

Say: **When we have Jesus in our hearts, we have great joy and happiness because we know that we have an eternal home in heaven with Jesus. We can still have that joy in our hearts even when times are difficult or sad. The joy is permanent because Jesus is permanently in our hearts. Let's play a game to remind us that we can have joy at all times.**

Have children stand in a row, shoulder to shoulder. Stand behind the finish line. Open your Bible to Philippians 4:4.

Say: **The Bible tells us to "Rejoice in the Lord, always." That means we should rejoice in good times and bad times, happy times and sad times, comfortable times and scary times. We can rejoice in Jesus' love no matter what our situation is.**

Lead children in this game, which is similar to Mother, May I. Offer a negative or positive statement to each child, such as, "You get one of your favorite cookies for dessert," or "You fell and skinned your knee." Regardless of whether the statement is positive or negative, have the child move forward in a positive way. For example, you could say, "Rejoice in the Lord with two hops" or "Take one joyful leap forward."

Have the child respond, "Rejoice in the Lord always!" and then carry out the action. Continue to call out similar situations and activities, to one child at a time, so that all kids cross the finish line at about the same time. When the last child crosses the line, have all the children say together: "Rejoice in the Lord always!"

Ask: • **Is it hard to be joyful when bad things happen? Explain.**

• **Why can we always be joyful?**

SOUVENIRS (10 to 15 minutes)
Joyful Friends

Children will create pictures that remind them to share their joy with others.

Say: We've talked a lot today about our hearts overflowing with joy. When we have that much joy, it makes us want to share it with others. We're going to make a souvenir page for our Travel Journals to remind us of ways we can share the joy of Jesus with others.

Give each child a copy of the "Joyful Friends" handout (p. 34), and have kids put their names on their handouts. Direct children to exchange papers. Let each child draw a picture of a way to share the joy of Jesus with others on the friend's paper. Then have children exchange papers again, so no one has his or her own paper, and each draw another picture, showing how to share the joy found in Jesus. Continue this process until the papers get too crowded for more pictures.

Say: You've done a great job of sharing your pictures and your joy with one another today. We've learned how 🔄 knowing Jesus gives us joy. Now let's go out and share God's joy with others.

Items to Pack: photocopies of "Joyful Friends" handouts, markers

FUN FACT There's a small town in Georgia named Hopeulikit, pronounced, "Hope you like it."

HOME AGAIN PRAYER (5 minutes)

Help children say this prayer and perform the accompanying motions.

Dear God,

Help me to have joy (place hands over heart and smile)

When things are going great. (Nod head.)

Help me to be happy (smile)

From town to city to state. (Point to various corners of the room.)

Help me to have joy (place hands over heart and smile)

When things are not just right. (Shake head and frown.)

Help me to be happy (smile)

From morning (hold hands over head in a circle) until night. (Hold hands in "prayer" fashion, lay head on hands like on a pillow, lean head, and close eyes.)

Help me to have joy (place hands over heart and smile)

Because I belong to you. (Point up.)

Help me to be happy (smile)

Through and through and through! (Touch head and then slide hand down body, bending over to touch toes.)

Amen.

JOYFUL FRIENDS

Peace

Pathway Point:  We can replace worry with peace because God is on our side.

In-Focus Verse: "Do not be anxious about anything, but in everything, by prayer and petition, with thanksgiving, present your requests to God. And the peace of God, which transcends all understanding, will guard your hearts and your minds in Christ Jesus" (Philippians 4:6-7).

Travel Itinerary

In their book *Millennials Rising,* Neil Howe and William Strauss describe the most recent generation as having more opportunities for prosperity and achievement than any other generation since the boomers. However, it seems that each new positive trend has a potential anxiety-generating underside that we should be diligent to shepherd our children through. The theme of sheltering our children has taken center stage in our cultural and political discourse. However, the increase in divorce rates and in the frequency of cohabitation has many children coping with the insecurity of living in fragile family systems. On a positive note, our children are more team-oriented and they value cooperation. However, play has become increasingly scheduled and organized with the rise of kids' sports leagues, and competitiveness has become more inherent in play. This generation values education and generally has a positive attitude toward school. However, the public education system's increased emphasis on standardized testing has significantly increased students' homework loads from a decade ago.

Many "peace robbers" exist in our culture. However, we know the key to having peace in every circumstance. Use this journey to teach children that no matter what pressures they face, they can find peace in their relationships with God through Jesus and his loving care of his children.

DEPARTURE PRAYER	(5 minutes)

In this activity, children will make pingpong ball prayers.

Items to Pack: pingpong balls, markers

Prayer is the prerequisite to peace. Calling out to God when they're anxious is one of the most foundational skills kids need to learn as children of God. To begin this journey, try this prayer activity. Give each child a pingpong ball. Ask kids to hold their pingpong balls and each write one thing on the ball that they sometimes worry about.

Say: **Dear God, many things worry us and make us feel anxious inside. You ask us to tell you about our problems and give them to you. We know you can take care of these problems. Thank you. Amen.** Have kids roll their pingpong balls as far from the group as they can.

1st STOP DISCOVERY (10 minutes) Tug of Warrior

Children will win an unfair Tug of War game to learn that God is on their side.

Place a tape line in the middle of the floor. Organize kids into two groups for a game of Tug of War. Place all the bigger and stronger kids on one side of the line and the younger children on the other side. Tell kids that they may not wrap the rope around their arms or wrists. Say: **We're going to play Tug of War. The team that drags any member of the opposite team across the tape line wins.**

Ask: • **Who do you think will win? Why?**

Join the team with the younger children, begin the game, and help the team with the younger children win. Make certain you pull slowly so no one gets hurt. Ask: • **Why didn't the game turn out the way you expected?**

Ask children on the younger team: • **Before you realized that I would help you, how did you feel about the game?**

• **Did you think the game was fair? Why or why not?**

• **Have you ever had to face a problem that you thought was too much for you to handle? How did you feel?**

• **How did you feel when you saw me join your team? Did it change how you felt? Why?**

• **How is God's being on our side like me joining one of the teams?**

Say: **Sometimes we get worried when a problem seems too big for us or is beyond our control to change. We may panic if we forget that God is on our side.**

We're learning about the fruit of the Spirit. We've explored how the fruit of the Spirit helps us love and have joy. Another quality of the fruit of the Spirit is peace. Let's look at someone in the Bible who learned to trade his worries for peace, because he learned someone big was on his side.

(15 to 20 minutes)
Chariots of Fire

Children will perform a creative re-enactment of 2 Kings 6.

Ask one volunteer to be Elisha and another to be Elisha's servant. Have Elisha's servant wear the sunglasses. Hand out foot-long pieces of crepe paper to each child. Have kids hide the crepe paper in their pockets. Instruct children to form a circle, and have the kids who are playing Elisha and his servant sit in the middle of the circle.

Open your Bible to 2 Kings 6. Say: **Our Bible story is from 2 Kings 6. In our story, an evil king sent his army to kill Elisha. God had used Elisha to keep the evil king from hurting God's people. So the king thought that if he could just kill Elisha, then he would be able to hurt God's people. The king sent his armies to surround the city so Elisha could not escape. Elisha's servant looked out the window and saw chariots and horses circling the city.**

Have the rest of the children pretend to ride horses and gallop around Elisha and his servant. Encourage them to whoop and make war cries.

After kids circle Elisha and his servant, have them sit down. Ask: • **How do you think Elisha and his servant felt? Why?**

Hand out the self-stick notes and pencils. Have kids each write one thing that worries them. Have them stick their notes on the lenses of the servant's sunglasses.

Ask: • **How does worrying keep us from seeing things as they are?**

• **What do we tend to focus on when we're worried?**

Say: Elisha's servant was very worried. He saw all the armies and worried. There were only two people against all those armies. He could not feel any peace because he was imagining all the bad things he thought would happen to him. Elisha, on the other hand, was very peaceful. He was calm and did not panic. The armies that wanted to hurt him did not seem to worry him at all.

Ask: • **Whose reaction seems to make sense—the servant and his worried reaction or Elisha and his peaceful reaction? Why?**

• **Why do you think Elisha had peace?**

• **What does it mean to have peace?**

Say: **Elisha felt peace inside because he could see something no one else could see.** Have children pull the crepe paper strips from their pockets and wave them. Say: **Elisha saw that the mountain was full of horses and chariots of fire. These were God's angels sent to protect them. Elisha could be peaceful**

SCENIC ROUTE → For a snack, try dyeing vanilla pudding with red food coloring to remind children of the fiery chariots. Let kids dip vanilla wafer "chariot wheels" into the pudding and enjoy.

Items to Pack: Construction paper, scissors, markers, tape or a stapler

in the face of danger because he knew God was near, giving his protection. Elisha prayed that God would open the eyes of his servant. Have Elisha's servant take off the sunglasses.

Ask: • **When is it hard to remember that God is near and that he wants to help us?**

• **What can we do to remember that God is here to help us?**

Say: The servant's eyes were opened. He saw God's chariots. He also saw God blind the eyes of the enemies. None of the enemies could see a thing. Elisha could be peaceful and calm because he knew that God was big enough to take care of everything.

ADVENTURES IN GROWING

(10 minutes)
Breakout

Children will make paper-chain worries then break out of them.

Before class cut several pieces of construction paper into two-inch strips.

Hand out several strips of construction paper to each child. Instruct kids to each write or draw one thing that they worry about on each strip. Show children how to make paper chains with the links by looping the paper strips and fastening the ends together with a stapler or tape. Help kids link the ends around their wrists to look like handcuffs.

Ask: • **How can worrying be like being stuck in a pair of handcuffs?**

• **How do you feel on the inside when you worry?**

Say: When we worry and become afraid, it's like being chained up. We can be too afraid to do things that we know make God happy. Instead of being peaceful and free, we can become fearful and not do anything. The good news is that ⬤ we can have peace because God is on our side.

On the count of three, have children shout, "Greater is he that is in [me] than he that is in the world" (1 John 4:4). Have the children pull their arms apart and break their chains.

SOUVENIRS → (15 to 20 minutes)
Peaceful Pictures

Children will use melted crayons to create the scene from 2 Kings 6 for their Travel Journals.

Before class cut three thirteen-inch pieces of wax paper for each child. Set up an ironing board in the corner of the room, in a low traffic area. Ten minutes before this segment of the lesson, set the iron on a low-temperature setting and make sure children stay away from the iron.

Say: **Let's make a scene from our Bible story to help us remember it.** Hand out a copy of the "Unfair Advantage" handout (p. 42) to each child. Point out the soldier in the center of the page. Say: **Elisha's servant was afraid of the soldiers. He was worried about all the bad things the soldiers could do to hurt him. Use a pencil to write on the shield of the mean soldier one thing that you find yourself worrying about a lot.**

Give children a moment to write. Show kids how to use the crayon sharpeners or plastic knives to make piles of red, yellow, and orange crayon shavings. Have each child place a copy of the "Unfair Advantage" handout between two pieces of wax paper. Have kids place crayon shavings over the chariots that they want to turn into fiery chariots, and then each place their last sheet of wax paper over the top of the other two sheets of paper. Say: **The crayon shavings remind us of the fire that Elisha's servant saw on the chariots of God. Seeing God's power helped the servant share Elisha's peaceful confidence in God.**

Ask: • **Can you think of other Bible stories in which God shows his mighty power?**

• **How does it feel to remember that God is powerful and can handle anything that worries us?**

• **How does remembering God's power help us experience peace?**

Carefully carry a child's "stack" to the ironing board. Move the iron in a circular motion over the wax paper to melt the crayon shavings and to fuse the sheets of wax paper. When everyone has finished, say: **Elisha was calm and peaceful because he saw God's chariots and knew that God was powerful.**

Ask: • **How can we remember God's power?**

• **When is it easy to remember his power?**

• **When is it hard to believe that God is powerful and can help us overcome our worries?**

• **What can you do to have peace when you're worried?**

HOME AGAIN PRAYER (5 minutes)

Turn off the classroom lights, and if possible, draw the window shades. Turn on the lamp. Instruct children to stand in front of the lamp and make scary shadows on the wall.

Items to Pack: wax paper; scissors; iron; ironing board or several bath-sized towels; copies of the "Unfair Advantage" handout (p. 42); several old red, yellow, and orange crayons; several crayon sharpeners or plastic knives; pencils

TOUR GUIDE TIP Be sure children use the pencils and not the crayons to write their worries. The hot iron will destroy any crayon handwriting, and the craft will lose some of its effectiveness to remind students of how God can provide them with peace in the situations they face.

FUN FACT The three-toed sloth moves at a peaceful rate of .06 miles per hour. Nothing seems to rush this guy!

Items to Pack: A floor or table lamp with a strong bulb, a flashlight, a Bible

Ask: • How do these shadows compare with what you actually look like?

• Are these shadows bigger or smaller than you are? Why?

• How are these shadows like the things that worry us?

Turn on the room lights. Encourage children again to make scary shadows.

Ask: • Do your shadows seem as scary now? Why or why not?

• How is God like the strong room light?

• How can remembering God's power help us have peace?

• Why is it important to have peace?

Say: When we choose to worry instead of remembering God's power, it's like being in a dark room with just a little light. Our worries are like giant shadows. But when we stop, pray, and take time to remember God's power, it's like turning the lights on in the room. Our problems seem a lot smaller. Worrying makes it hard to see that God is powerful and wants to help us in our hard times. That's when we lose our peace. But God says we can trade in our worries for his perfect peace.

Turn the room lights out, and turn on the flashlight. Pray: **God, we thank you that you are always with us and are on our side. Knowing this gives us peace. Sometimes we get worried and stop seeing that you are with us. Help us see that you are on our side so we'll be able to stop worrying.**

Open your Bible to Philippians 4:6-7. Say: **Philippians 4:6-7 says, "Do not be anxious about anything, but in everything, by prayer and petition, with thanksgiving, present your requests to God. And the peace of God, which transcends all understanding, will guard your hearts and your minds in Christ Jesus."**

Ask: • What does it mean to be anxious?

• Why do you think it's important for us to be thankful?

Say: There are a couple of big words in this verse. A "petition" is when you ask someone important for help. The phrase "which transcends all understanding" means that God promises to give us more peace so that we're calm even when it doesn't seem to make sense—just as Elisha was peaceful even when the army surrounded him.

Ask: • What do you think it means that God's peace guards our hearts and minds?

• How do you feel knowing that God promises to give us peace from all our worries?

Say: God says he'll trade our worries for his peace. All we have to do is ask for God's help with the things that rob us of our peace. I'm going to pass

TOUR GUIDE TIP Some children may not feel comfortable sharing their worries. Allow children to say, "God, I give you my worries."

TOUR GUIDE TIP For this activity, you can tape large black garbage bags to the windows to help block out sunlight. Tape the bags directly to the glass because some tapes can pull the paint from wall surfaces.

SCENIC ROUTE Let kids look through a pair of old prescription glasses, a glass of water, or a kaleidoscope. Explain how each of these changes how we see things. Discuss how worry distorts how we see reality and robs us of our peace.

the flashlight around the circle. When you hold the flashlight, tell God one thing that worries you. Then say, "Please give me your peace."

Pass the flashlight around the circle. When the flashlight returns to you, pray: God, thank you for guarding over our hearts and our minds with your peace. We praise you for being powerful enough to handle everything that worries us. We love you. Amen.

A mother alligator sometimes carries her babies around in her mouth. It's the safest place in the world for these babies.

Unfair Advantage

Patience

Pathway Point: 🥧 We should be patient with others in the same way that God is patient with us.

In-Focus Verse: "Be patient, then, brothers, until the Lord's coming" (James 5:7a).

Travel Itinerary

Impatience seems to be a standard feature of childhood. As children advance through their developmental tasks, they see the next step and often can't wait to take it. It starts with an irate two-year-old who can't reach the cookies on the table and ends...never.

The root of impatience is stymied goals—it doesn't matter whether the source of the resistance is within the person or comes from someone else. Impatient reactions are protests that someone's agenda is being violated. Behind all impatience is a self-centered idea that "I am the most important and everyone surrounding me is a prop to help me meet my goals." We can challenge this egocentric thinking with the example of God, who forgave us at a great price, even when our sinful behavior blocked his goal of intimate friendship with us.

DEPARTURE PRAYER	(5 minutes)

Children will look at a rabbit and turtle as prayer starters.

Items to Pack: picture of a rabbit, picture of a turtle

Hold up the picture of the hare.

Ask: • **If you could put a jackrabbit on a leash and take it for a walk, what would it be like?**

• **How tired would you be after the walk? Why?**

Hold up the picture of the turtle.

Ask: • **What would it be like to take a turtle for a walk? Why?**

• **How would you feel after walking the turtle?**

Say: Turtles are famous for being slow. **If you had to wait for a turtle to walk anywhere, you would need a lot of patience.**

Ask: • **Can you think of some real-life examples of situations in which you need lots of patience?**

• **Is it easy or hard to be patient? Why?**

• **Why is it important to be patient?**

Say: **We all get impatient sometimes. Sometimes it's hard to wait on people**

SCENIC ROUTE This activity will make a greater impact if you can borrow a pet turtle and rabbit.

43

for things to happen. Sometimes people do things that bother us. It's easy to get grouchy with other people when we feel impatient. But God wants us to treat other people well, even when they do things that bug us. That's why we need this fruit of the Spirit. Pass the picture of a turtle around the group as you say this prayer.

Pray: Dear God, sometimes we get impatient with other people. We get mad when people don't do things our way or if they're not fast enough. Please help us learn how to be patient. In Jesus' name, amen.

1st STOP DISCOVERY (10 minutes) Going Bananas

Children will pass a banana along a line to learn about patience.

Have kids stand in a straight line. Say: **Let's see how fast we can pass a banana up and back down the line. Here is the catch: You can't use your hands. You must hold the banana with your chin. Pass the banana, chin to chin, up and down the line. If someone drops the banana, you must start over.**

Place the banana beneath the chin of the child in front of the line. Show that child how to hold the banana between his or her chin and chest. Odds are that the banana will drop to the floor a few times during the game. Allow children to express frustration, but redirect unkind words. If children have an especially difficult time, modify the rules so kids can restart the game with the same partner who dropped the banana.

When kids have finished, gather them around you in a circle.

Ask: • **Was this game easy or difficult for you? Why?**

• **How did you feel when someone dropped the banana? Why?**

• **If you dropped the banana, how did you feel when you heard the group's reaction?**

Say: **It's easy to feel impatient when things don't go your way. Sometimes people do things that make it hard for you to get what you want. When we get impatient, we're tempted to say things that aren't nice. We can make others feel bad. Today we're going to learn about an important fruit of the Spirit—patience.** 🕐 **And we'll explore how we should be patient with others in the same way that God is patient with us.**

Items to Pack: banana

TOUR GUIDE TIP
When you create the line, have children line up next to someone close to their own height. This will help kids pass the banana.

SCENIC ROUTE →
For extra fun, play slow-motion relays in which the goal is to be the slowest team. Have children try hopping, skipping, or running as slowly as they can.

(20 minutes)

First National Bank of Patience

Items to Pack: Bible, large bag of pennies; two emptied and cleaned plastic, gallon milk jugs; razor knife; string or yarn; hole punch; yardstick; chair with a flat back; duct tape; scissors; yellow construction paper; tape

Before class, make a pair of measuring scales. To make the buckets of the scales, cut the top half from two milk jugs. Punch a hole in each of the four corners of the bottom half of each jug. Measure and cut eight pieces of string. Thread a string through each of the holes in the milk jugs and tie a secure knot. With each jug, join the four loose ends of the strings in a knot. Make sure that each length of string is close to the same length below the knot. Make a crown from the yellow construction paper.

Set a chair in the center of the room. Balance the yardstick on the back of the chair. Hang the buckets from opposite ends of the yardstick, and use a piece of duct tape to secure the string to the yardstick and to secure the stick to the chair so it can easily move up and down.

Gather children near your balance scales. Open your Bible to Matthew 18 and say: **In Bible times, people used scales to weigh out gold when people bought or sold things. Our story in the Bible has a *lot* of money in it. These scales will help us understand the story. One day Peter asked Jesus how many times he needed to show patience and forgiveness to someone who kept sinning against him. Peter asked if seven times was enough.**

Ask: **• Did you ever have someone do the same rotten thing to you again and again?**

• How did you feel about that person?

• Is it easy or hard to be patient with someone who repeatedly does things to hurt you? Why?

• What would showing patience to that person look like?

Say: **I'll tell you how many times Jesus told Peter that he needed to show patience in a little bit. Right now let's look at the story that Jesus told Peter about being patient.** Choose one child to be the king and two others to be the king's servants. Place a second chair near the scales, and designate it as the king's throne. Have the king sit on the throne and wear the crown.

One day the king was looking at his money books. He realized that one of his servants owed him 10,000 talents of gold. Today 10,000 talents of gold probably would be worth millions of dollars!

Ask: **• What would you do with that much money if someone loaned it to you?**

• How would you feel if you had all that money?

• How long do you think you would have to work to earn that much money to pay the person back?

TOUR GUIDE TIP If you can't gather enough coins, use marbles or something else that will tip the scales you've made.

45

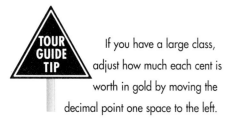

If you have a large class, adjust how much each cent is worth in gold by moving the decimal point one space to the left.

Pour out the bag of coins on the floor. Say: **Let's pretend that each penny is the same as 5,000 pounds of gold. That means we'll need 150 pennies for 750,000 pounds of gold. Work as a class to count out "750,000 pounds of gold."**

Let the class work together to count out the money. After they've counted the money, have kids place it in one bucket of the scales.

Say: **The servant did not have that much money.** Have the child playing the first servant turn his or her pockets inside out. Say: **The king ordered that the servant and his whole family be sold into slavery to pay off the debt. The king also ordered that everything the servant owned be sold.**

Ask: • **How do you think the servant felt?**

• **What would you do if you were the servant?**

Have children give the "servant" suggestions for what to do and say. Have the child act out the suggestions.

Say: **The servant begged the king to have mercy on him. The king felt sorry for him and forgave him all the money he owed.**

Ask: • **How do you think the servant felt to be forgiven of all that money?**

• **What do you think he did?**

Say: **The first servant went out and found a second servant.** (Have the second servant stand next to the first servant.) **The second servant owed the first one a couple of months' worth of pay.** Have a child place a few coins on the second side of the scales.

Ask: • **Remember, the first servant was just forgiven for a debt that he would never be able to repay. What do you think he said and did to the second servant?**

Have your volunteers act out the following scene. Say: **The second servant begged the first servant to be patient with him and to just give him a little more time. This was a debt the second servant should have been able to pay if he just had a few months to work. The first servant refused to have patience. He grabbed the servant and threw him in jail until he could repay him. When the king found out, he was furious. He threw the first servant in jail until he could repay the king in full.**

Ask: • **What is surprising about the way the first servant treated the second servant?**

• **Do you think that the king's reaction was fair? Why or why not?**

• **How is the king like God?**

• **How is the king different from God?**

Say: **The Bible says when we do something wrong to someone, it's like owing that person money.**

For extra fun, bring in three bathrobes or biblical costumes for the actors to wear.

Ask: • Who do we owe more to than anyone else?

• Why is it so important to have patience with other people?

Say: God shows us patience every day. He is patient with us when we sin. He is patient with us when we are slow to do the things we know would make God happy. All of these things add up every day, making us like that first servant who owed God more money than he could ever repay. God expects us to imitate his patience by forgiving others when they do bad things to us and by being kind when others make us wait. ◑ We should be patient with others in the same way that God is patient with us.

ADVENTURES IN GROWING

(10 minutes)
Patience Charades

Before class make a copy of the "Patience Pantomime" cards (p. 50), and cut the cards apart.

Say: We need patience so many times every day! I'm going to pantomime a situation in which you would need to use patience. When you think you know what I'm doing, call it out. If you're right, you can either make up and act out your own situation that calls for patience or choose a "Patience Pantomime" card and act out that situation.

Items to Pack: "Patience Pantomime" cards (p. 50), scissors, pencil, index cards

Draw a "Patience Pantomime" card, and act out the situation. When a child has guessed what you're acting out, allow the child to either make up a situation in which patience is needed or draw a card. If a child makes up his or her own situation to act out, write that situation on an index card before the next round. If a child guesses correctly more than one situation, have that child select a child to have a turn who has not had a chance to pantomime. Collect all of the "Patience Pantomime" cards and the situations written on the index cards, and reserve them for the next activity.

Ask: • Why do you think patience is so important in all the situations we've acted out?

• Did you have to have patience when you were acting out your situation? when you were trying to guess?

• Why is it sometimes hard to have patience?

TOUR GUIDE TIP If a child needs help thinking of how to act out a situation or needs another person to help mime, let the child choose one or two other children to help.

(5 minutes)
Patience-o-Meters

Children will further explore the situations they looked at in the pantomiming exercise.

Use a marker to number the plates from 1 to 5. Place the paper plates across

Items to Pack: Five paper plates, marker, list of situations the children chose from the "Patience Charades" activity

Items to Pack: copies of "Patience in the Balance" handout (p. 51), colored card stock for each child, scissors, brass paper fasteners, glue

the room, evenly spaced from one another in a line. Read one of the situations from the "Patience Charades" activity. Say: **If it would be hard for you to be patient in this situation, stand next to Plate 5. If this situation wouldn't test your patience at all, stand next to Plate 1. If you are somewhere in between, stand next to the number closest to how hard you think it would be for you to be patient.**

Give students time to move to the appropriate plate.

Ask: • **Would any of you like to share why you chose the number you did?** Repeat the activity until all the situations have been read.

Ask: • **Why is it easier to be patient in some situations than in others?**

• **Why should we work at being patient?**

• **How can we remind ourselves to be patient when we don't feel like it?**

Say: **Sometimes it's easy to be patient, and sometimes having to wait on someone is hard. Or sometimes someone does something bad to us and we get mad. The times it's hard for us to be forgiving are when we *need* God's help to be patient. We need to stop, calm ourselves, and remember the big debt we owe God and how he is patient with us. When we do this, it's easier to show patience to others.** 🕐 **Remember, we should be patient with others in the same way that God is patient with us. God's Word encourages us to be patient, as we wait for Jesus' coming. Let's practice some ways of doing that now.**

SOUVENIRS → (10 minutes)
In the Balance

Children will create scales as reminders of how patient God is with us. Kids will add these pages to their Travel Journals.

Say: **In our Bible story, we learned that the things for which God is patient with us far outweigh anything that we need to be patient for. Let's make a set of scales to remind us of how great God's patience is with us.**

Hand out scissors. Have children cut out the base of the pendulum from the "Patience in the Balance" handout (p. 51) and glue it to the center of a piece of card stock. Next have children cut out the arm of the scales with the two buckets. Show kids how to use a paper fastener to fasten the center of the arm of the scales so that the arm teeters on the fulcrum.

Say: **I want you to think of all the things that people do to you that make you impatient. Now tip the scales toward the right side. Now think of all the things for which God has been patient with you. Now tip the scales to the left. God is so patient with our sins. We're like the servant who owed the** king millions of dollars. God is patient and forgiving with us. He wants us to be patient with others just as he is patient and forgiving with us.

HOME AGAIN PRAYER (5 minutes)

Children will make impressions of coins as reminders to be patient.

Items to Pack: paper, sack of pennies, crayons

Give each child a few coins. Instruct kids to set their coins on the table in front of them, and have each child cover the coins with a blank piece of paper. Say: **Sometimes we forget how much we owe God. We forget how patient he is with us. When we forget God's patience with us, we act like the bad servant and we stop being patient with others. We need to remember the big debt we owe God. The bad things we do caused God to send his Son, Jesus, to die on the cross to take away our sins. We can never begin to repay that debt. We need to remember how loving and patient God is with us.**

Show children how to rub a crayon on the paper over the coins so they see impressions of the coins on the paper.

Pray: **Dear God, thank you for being so patient with us. We owe you more than we can repay. Help us remember how much we owe you and how patient you are with us.** ◑ **We choose to be patient with others the way you are patient with us. In Jesus' name, amen.**

49

Patience Pantomimes

Card 1:

It's time for your softball game. You need to be there in fifteen minutes. Your mother is on the phone and doesn't seem to be in a big hurry to get you there on time. The team needs you.

Card 2:

Your baby brother wandered into your room and ripped up your favorite book.

Card 3:

Your best friend told an embarrassing story about you again. She had *promised* she would never do it again. Now she says she's really sorry and will never do it again.

Card 4:

Bobby is on your soccer team. He isn't very good. He keeps messing up. You keep losing games because of him. You hate losing.

Card 5:

You have to walk your little sister to school. She is such a slowpoke. You want to get to school early so you have time to talk to your friends.

Card 6:

Your dad promised he would take you fishing after he fixed the car. That was hours ago. Dad is still in the garage, and if you wait too much longer, the fish will not be biting anymore.

Card 7:

You agreed to tutor a younger child at school. You're trying to explain to Bobby how to do a simple math problem. But Bobby doesn't get it. It doesn't seem like he is even trying. You're getting frustrated.

Card 8:

You're trying to learn a difficult song on the piano. You keep messing up. You've been practicing and practicing. You just can't seem to get it.

Patience in the Balance

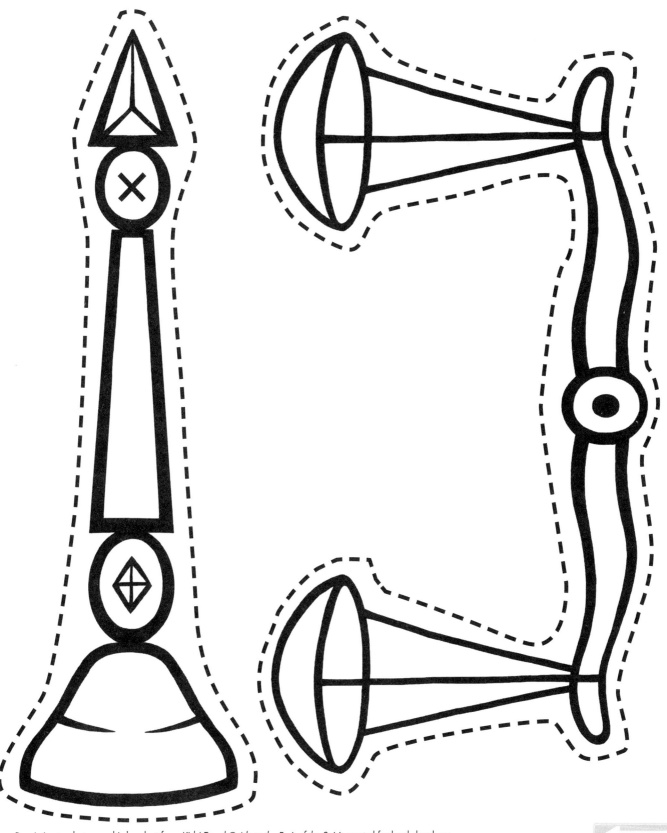

Kindness

Pathway Point: 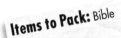 Be kind to everyone.

In-Focus Verse: "Make sure that nobody pays back wrong for wrong, but always try to be kind to each other and to everyone else" (1 Thessalonians 5:15).

Travel Itinerary

Children naturally want things their way, and they are still learning to put others first. A sister may be very quick to say, "My brother won't share with me," when the brother begins to play with a toy that she decides looks inviting. This journey strives to teach children to sympathize with other people and to understand others' feelings, putting others first rather than continuously thinking of their own personal needs or satisfaction. This journey encourages children to be kind to others at all times.

Items to Pack: Bible

DEPARTURE PRAYER	(5 minutes)

Children will pray about "clothing" themselves with kindness.

Say: **On our journey today, we'll learn about another fruit of the Spirit quality—kindness. Galatians 5:22-23a tells us, "But the fruit of the Spirit is love, joy, peace, patience, kindness, goodness, faithfulness, gentleness and self-control." "Kindness"—did you hear that word? Let's talk about how we can show kindness to others at all times.**

Ask: • **Can you tell me one of the first things you do when you wake up in the morning?**

Say: One of the first things we do in the morning to get ready for the day is to put on our clothes. Our clothes cover or surround our bodies. Listen to what God says in his Word: "Therefore, as God's chosen people, holy and dearly loved, clothe yourselves with compassion, kindness, humility, gentleness and patience." That's from Colossians 3:12.

Ask: • **What do you think it means to "clothe yourself" with compassion and kindness?**

Say: Just as our clothes surround and cover our bodies, kindness can surround us. God wants us to cover ourselves with kindness, to have kindness from our heads to our toes, so that we can show that kindness to other people.

◐ **Let's act out this prayer as we "dress ourselves" in kindness.**

Have kids repeat this prayer after you, line by line, pretending to put on each mentioned article of clothing.

> **Dear God,**
>
> **My shirt goes right on top.**
>
> **Let kind deeds never stop.**
>
> **I'll put my pants on next.**
>
> **Help me to act my best.**
>
> **Here are socks for my feet.**
>
> **Make my words sound sweet.**
>
> **Last, I'll put on shoes.**
>
> **Let kindness be my rule.**
>
> **Clothe me with kindness and love.**
>
> **Thank you, God above.**
>
> **Amen.**

TOUR GUIDE TIP If you work with older kids, let them work in pairs. Have each pair choose an article of clothing and write a verse for the poem. Put all the verses together, read them aloud, and have kids act out dressing accordingly.

1st STOP DISCOVERY (20 minutes) Station K-I-N-D

Kids will take turns acting out situations in a kind manner and in a mean manner to determine which way is more Christlike.

Items to Pack: Bibles, television or VCR remote control

Before class move tables and chairs to allow room for children to act. Have kids form small groups to perform the following scenes, making sure that each child gets to act at least once. Have the remote control handy. Ask children to turn to 2 Timothy 2:24 and follow along as you read. Have children who do not have Bibles form pairs with children who do, or provide Bibles from the classroom.

Say: **2 Timothy 2:24a says, "And the Lord's servant must not quarrel; instead, he must be kind to everyone." God wants us to be kind to each and every person. We're going to pretend that we're actors at two television stations. One station is called Station K-I-N-D, Kind, and the other station is called Station M-E-A-N, Mean. I'll bet you can guess what's going to happen at each station!**

Use the following situations or make up your own. Form five groups of children, using the situations as a guide for the number of children needed. Give each group one of the situations to act out, and allow kids time to discuss how they will act. After children have practiced their scenes, have all but kids from the first group sit on the floor. Have the first group act out its situation in a kind manner. For example, for Situation 1, the child holding the video game could respond with a comment such as, "Oh, I'm sorry. I should have asked first to borrow your game. Please forgive me." And the other child responds, "That's all right. I shouldn't have yelled at you. Of course you may play my game. May I have a turn when you've finished?"

After the group has finished acting out the scene in a kind manner, give the remote control to someone on the floor and ask the person to "change the channel" to Station M-E-A-N. Then have the group act out the scene in an unkind manner. For example, in Situation 1, the two children could pretend to fight over the video game, drop the game, and break it. After both scenes have been acted out for a situation, ask the questions below. Then continue with the next situation and a new group of kids.

Ask: • **Which set of actors behaved in a Christlike manner?**

• **How do you think the people felt in the unkind scenes?**

• **Can you tell me about a time something like this happened to you?**

Situation 1: One child is playing a hand-held video game. His or her sister walks in and says, "Hey, that's my game!"

Situation 2: Two children are playing at the park. Another child sits alone with no one to play with.

Situation 3: Two children from the same family decide to eat a snack. Both children want apples to eat. Only one apple is left.

Situation 4: Two children are watching a favorite television show. Mom asks the children to clean their rooms because one of her friends is on her way over for a visit.

Situation 5: Dad is busy collecting trash for the garbage pickup. Three children are playing Frisbee in the yard when Dad comes by with an armload of trash bags.

SCENIC ROUTE → To make the situations seem more realistic, bring in dress-up clothes and props for each situation, such as a hand-held video, basket with only one apple, and a Frisbee.

Items to Pack: Bible

STORY EXCURSION (5 to 10 minutes)
All-Day Kindness

Say: **The Bible tells us in Ephesians 4:32a, "Be kind and compassionate to one another."** We can be kind to someone by saying nice words to that person. **Give me an example of kind words that you could say to a person.** (Pause to allow responses.) **We can also be kind to a person by doing a kind deed for that person. Give me an example of a kind deed.** (Pause to allow responses.) **We can also be kind by thinking kind thoughts. Give me an example of a kind thought that you have had today about someone in this room.** (Pause for responses.)

Now, we're going to go through a pretend day. We'll start from the time we get up in the morning and see just how many kind things we can think, say, or do. We want to learn to be kind from the moment we get up until the moment we fall asleep at night. 🕐 God wants us to be kind at all times.

Choose a partner who you want to discuss kind words or deeds with, and sit near that partner. I'll have you share with your partner during the story. Now let's start our day.

Stretch really big and rub your eyes as if you just woke up. You're still sleepy because you stayed up too late watching the cartoon channel on television. Your sister or brother walks into your room and says, "Good morning," in a very cheerful voice. Tell your partner some kind words that you could say to your sister or brother. (Pause briefly.) If you thought of something to say other than "Good morning," raise your hand and let's share those kind words with the rest of the class. Encourage children with raised hands to respond.

Say: You walk to the kitchen where your mom is preparing your favorite breakfast. Close your eyes and pretend to smell your favorite breakfast. Open your eyes, and share with your partner some kind thoughts that you might have at this very minute. (Pause.) Now share the kind words that you will say to your mom. (Pause.)

After you eat, you notice that your baby brother has spilled cereal pieces on the floor. Tell your partner what kind deed you can do. (Pause.) Your mom is still busy in the kitchen. Think for a minute about what kind thing you could do next. Share this with your partner. (Pause.)

Later in the morning, your younger sister asks you to play her favorite game, a game you used to like but now you prefer another game. Share with your partner kind words and kind deeds you could say and do. (Pause.)

Ask: • How did you solve this problem in a kind way?

Say: After lunch, you meet one of your friends at the park. Think of a kind way to greet your friend. Share that with your partner. If you thought of a really cool way to say hello to your friend without using the word "hello," raise your hand and let's share that with the entire group. (Pause for responses.)

While you're playing with your friend, a new person comes to the park who you've never seen. His clothes are kind of dirty, and he doesn't have anyone to play with. Now tell your friend what kind thoughts you could have. (Pause.) What kind words might you say to your friend? What kind words could you say to the new kid? And what kind deed could you do?

SCENIC ROUTE →

To remind children to use words, thoughts, and actions to show kindness, teach the words of this song to the tune of "Battle Hymn of the Republic."

When your heart has Jesus, then there's kindness in your words.

When your heart has Jesus, then there's kindness in your thoughts.

When your heart has Jesus, then there's kindness in what you do.

Be kind; be kind; be kind.

Marching forward with our kindness.

Marching backward with our kindness.

Marching forward with our kindness.

Be kind; be kind; be kind.

At the dinner table, Dad puts a helping of vegetables that you do not like on your plate. Tell your friend what kind thought you could have. (Pause.) Now tell your friend what kind words you could say. (Pause.) And now what kind deed could you do? (Pause.)

It's almost bedtime. Let me see a big yawn! Your mom tells you to brush your teeth and clean your room. You'd really rather watch TV. Tell your partner a kind thought, kind words, and a kind deed that fit this part of your day. (Pause.)

When you've finished cleaning your room, you notice that your brother still has a lot of things to clean in his room. Think about what you could do to show kindness. Share your idea with your friend. (Pause.)

It's almost time to climb into bed. Think of kind words to say to each person in your family. Share these words with your partner, telling him or her just what you would say to each person. Try to think of something really special to say to each person. Give children enough time to share with their partners.

We've just shown kindness from sunup until sundown! When we have Jesus in our lives, we want to show kindness all the time. We can show kindness with our words, our thoughts, and our actions. This may not always be an easy job. We may be in a grouchy mood and really have to work at being kind. Or we may meet someone else who is grouchy, and it's often hard to be kind to someone who is especially rude or mean. By knowing Jesus and keeping him in our hearts, we can work hard at showing kindness all the time.

Items to Pack: Bible, coins

ADVENTURES IN GROWING

(15 minutes)
Kindness Coins

Open your Bible to 1 Thessalonians 5:15, and read the verse to the children. Give each child three coins. Have kids walk around the room and each say something kind to another person. The child who receives the kind comment will then "pay back" with a kind comment and a kindness coin. Kids will continue playing until they have given away all their coins and have each received three new coins from others.

For the second part of the game, ask for a volunteer to be "grouchy." Point out to kids that they will often meet people who are unkind. Remind them that we are instructed to be kind to others, even if they are grouchy or unkind. Have the grouchy child approach each child, one at a time, and make a grouchy comment. Some examples are, "Boy, what a yucky day! I hate the rain!" "This sandwich tastes horrible! I wish my mom would have made me a peanut butter and jelly sandwich instead!" or "Math is so boring! I'll be so glad when class is over!"

When the "grouchy child" makes an unkind comment, the other child will respond by speaking kindly and giving the grouchy person a coin. After each child has had a turn repaying the grouchy person with kind words, point out that the grouchy person is now "rich" with kind words. Then have the grouchy person end with a kind comment or kind act.

Say: **Our kind words can change a person's heart and make that person also want to be kind. It's easy to repay a kind comment with another kind comment. But it's a lot harder to repay a mean comment with a kind one!**

🌑 **God wants us to be kind to everyone. That's exactly why God has this to say to us: "Make sure that nobody pays back wrong for wrong, but always try to be kind to each other and to everyone else" (1 Thessalonians 5:15).**

(10 minutes)
Around the World With Kindness

Remind kids that God wants us to share the fruit of the Spirit with others. Show children a globe.

Ask: • **How can you be kind to the whole world?**

Say: **Let's make a friendship chain to see how we can be kind to the "whole world."**

Give each child a small strip of construction paper. Encourage each child to write one kind thing he or she can say or do. Next, have kids form pairs. Give pairs more paper strips, and encourage each pair to think of kind words or kind acts and write them, one idea per construction paper strip. Have each pair write at least two ideas, preferably more. As children think and work, walk around with a stapler. Tell each pair that they first showed kindness as individuals. Then by working in pairs, they showed kindness as a small town or community. Staple each pair's construction paper together in links, like a chain. When finished stapling, have kids form groups of four. As a foursome, kids will write other kind acts or kind words on construction paper strips, one idea per strip. Staple the new strips and the two chains together, forming a longer chain. Point out to each group that their kindnesses have now been spread to a whole country. Bring all the children together on the floor, and let them work together to brainstorm new kind ideas. Give each child another strip of construction paper to write the ideas on. Staple together all the new ideas and the other chains. Tell children that kind words and kind deeds have been stretched around the world. If your chain is long enough, have kids sit together closely on the floor and wrap the chain around the whole group. If the chain is not long enough to wrap around all the children, place the globe on the floor and wrap the chain around the globe.

Items to Pack: strips of construction paper, pens, stapler, globe

FUN FACT

Established in 1995, the Random Acts of Kindness Foundation is an organization for people dedicated to spreading kindness. This foundation encourages the celebration of World Kindness Day, November 13, celebrated by people in at least ten nations.

Items to Pack: photocopies of the "Kindness Brings a Smile" handout, (p. 59), black and yellow crayons

SOUVENIRS (5 minutes)
Kindness Brings a Smile

Photocopy the "Kindness Brings a Smile" handout (p. 59) for each child. Instruct each child to use a black crayon to circle the pictures that show kids doing unkind things and to completely color over the picture with black crayon. Next, have each child color in the rest of the large circle with yellow. When kids have completed their pages, they will resemble smiling faces. Remind children that when we show kindness to others, it makes us happy and it makes others happy. When kids have finished, instruct them to place the pages in their Travel Journals.

Items to Pack: gift wrap, empty box, tape

HOME AGAIN PRAYER (5 minutes)

Before class, gift-wrap an empty box. Have children sit in a circle. Give one child the gift. Have that child pass the gift to the next person and say the prayer below. After praying, have that child suggest a way he or she will be kind this week. The child holding the gift will now pass the gift to the next person, pray, and give a suggestion for a kind deed. Continue until each person has prayed.

Dear God, ◓ **Help me to give the gift of kindness to everyone I meet. Amen.**

TOUR GUIDE TIP   If you have a large group of children, wrap additional empty boxes and form several small groups.

Kindness Brings a Smile

Goodness

Pathway Point: We can grow in our goodness by staying close to God and remembering his goodness.

In-Focus Verse: "But just as he who called you is holy, so be holy in all you do" (1 Peter 1:15).

Travel Itinerary

"Goodness" is not a word that we use a lot today. We may see some things as good, such as when we say, "This pizza sure tastes *good"* or "I'm *good* at playing baseball!" But goodness carries a higher standard. Eugene Peterson translates the word "goodness" in *The Message* as "a conviction that a basic holiness permeates things and people."

The fruit of the Spirit quality of goodness is a characteristic of God's nature, and the challenge for believers is to live up to God's holiness. As children learn more about the Christian walk, they'll learn what it means to strive for holy lives.

Use this lesson to help children to grow closer to God and to look for ways to imitate God's goodness in their lives.

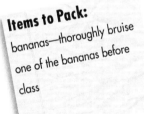

Items to Pack:
bananas—thoroughly bruise one of the bananas before class

| **DEPARTURE PRAYER** | (5 minutes) |

Offer a child the bruised banana as a snack. Let the child peel it.

Ask: • **Would you like to eat this snack? Why or why not?**

Peel a second banana, offer it to the child, and ask: • **Would you rather eat a banana like this?**

Say: **Jesus said you could know a tree by the kind of fruit it gives. Good fruit comes from good trees. Bad fruit comes from bad trees. Jesus was telling us that if we do good things, it's because we have his good Holy Spirit inside us to help us. Let's pray and ask God to help us give him good fruit.**

Have kids pass a good banana around the circle as you pray: **Dear God, you help us do good things. This is the fruit of your Holy Spirit helping us. Sometimes our friends don't do good. Help us to do the good thing even when we're the only ones doing what makes you happy. In Jesus' name, amen.**

TOUR GUIDE TIP Check to make sure your church has an up-to-date, blanket license that allows you to legally show movies.

1st STOP DISCOVERY (10 minutes)
A Tempting Treat

Before class, cue the video of *Willie Wonka and the Chocolate Factory* to the beginning of the scene in which the industrial spy tempts Charlie to smuggle out an Everlasting Gob-Stopper. The start time is forty minutes. The stop time is forty-two minutes.

Say: **It's not always easy to do good. Sometimes we get tempted. Let's watch a scene from *Willie Wonka and the Chocolate Factory*. This scene focuses on a boy named Charlie. Charlie and his family are very poor. Charlie has just won a ticket that earns him a spot on a tour of the mysterious Wonka Chocolate Factory. However, chances are that after the tour, things will go back to normal for Charlie and his family—unless something unusual happens. Let's see what that unusual thing could be.** Show the clip.

Ask: • **Do you think it's OK for Charlie to take one small Gob-Stopper from the factory when doing so will help his family? Why or why not?**

• **How would you feel if you were in Charlie's shoes and had a decision like this to make?**

• **What kind of advice would you give Charlie?**

Say: **Charlie had a chance to make his family comfortable for life. But he knew that he would have to do something that was not good. Stealing a tiny piece of candy doesn't seem like a big deal. However, Charlie knew that being good was very important.**

STORY EXCURSION (15 minutes)
Cooking Show

Ask three volunteers to read the script, "Cooking With Emerald" (p. 66).

To the rest of the class, say: **Listen carefully to the script. Anytime you hear the name "Daniel," I want you to shout, "We must do good." Anytime you hear Emerald the Cook say the word "Blammo!" I want you to raise your arms up and shout, "Punch it up!" It will be just like a cooking show.**

After kids have read the script, ask: • **How do you think Daniel and his friends felt when they had to stand up to Ashpenaz?**

• **Why do you think the other students from Judah did not stand up for what they knew was right?**

Items to Pack: television, VCR, and video of Willie Wonka and the Chocolate Factory

SCENIC ROUTE →

Reinforce today's food theme by having kids decorate the room to look like a restaurant. Offer them paper tablecloths, balloons, poster board, markers, paper plates, and plastic ware. Encourage kids to name their restaurant and prepare a menu of their favorite foods.

Items to Pack: Bible, copies of the "Cooking With Emerald" script (p. 66)

61

SCENIC ROUTE →

Bring in props such as a chef's hat, an apron, and kitchen utensils. Consider bringing in a camcorder to record the skit. As a fun means of review, you can play it back to the kids at the end of this class or at the beginning of the next class.

Items to Pack: chalkboard, chalk, chalkboard eraser, index cards, pencils, tape, Bible

FUN FACT

Through Nickelodeon's Big Help, kids get to show a lot of goodness. Every year, 40 million kids pledge almost 400 *million hours* of community service! If you had to work all those hours yourself, it'd take about 45,000 years.

• When is it hard for you to stand up for what's right?

• How do you think Daniel and his friends felt during the ten days?

Say: **Let's see what happened at the end of the ten days.** Read Daniel 1:15-17.

Ask: • **How did God honor Daniel and his friends for choosing to do what they knew was good?**

Say: Daniel and his friends did the right thing in their school even when no one else around them did. God is our Father and he is perfectly good. When we choose to do good things, it's a way of telling our Heavenly Father we want to be just like him. It's a way of showing love to God.

(10 to 15 minutes)
Never Forget

Say: Daniel and his friends could make a good decision because they remembered what God is like and what he says is good. Let's play a game to see how good our memories are.

Write the following words on the chalkboard—"house," "blender," "bagel," "avalanche," "piano," "football," "spaghetti," "monkey," "asteroid," "teacher," "pencil," "gravy," "bologna," and "not."

Say: **In a minute, I'm going to ask you to remember everything I've written on the board. Take a minute to study the words.**

Let kids look at the list for one minute. Thoroughly erase the chalkboard so it's impossible to make out what was written.

Say: **Now I'd like you all to sing the national anthem. After we sing, we'll see how well we recall our list.**

Lead kids in singing the national anthem. After they've finished, ask kids to tell you what the words were that had been on the chalkboard. Write their answers. After children have finished, write the words that they had forgotten.

Ask: **Was it easy or hard to remember the words? Why?**

• **Did singing the song make it easy or hard to remember the words?**

• **Are you surprised at how your group did at remembering the list of words? Why?**

• **Have you ever forgotten to do something important? How did you feel when you realized your mistake?**

Say: **You forgot some of the words because the song distracted you.** In our Bible story, the armies of Babylon had conquered Jerusalem and taken the brightest young men of Israel to Babylon. Daniel, Hananiah, Mishael, and Azariah were some of the captives. King Nebuchadnezzar wanted these men to serve him. King Nebuchadnezzar worshipped different gods and had different ideas about what it meant to be good. So he placed these young men in a special school for three years. He wanted God's people to forget about God so they would do what *he* thought was good.

The first thing King Nebuchadnezzar did to try to make the young men forget about God and his ways was to give them all different names.

Hand out index cards and pencils. Have children form pairs. Have each person think of a new name for his or her partner. Have each partner write the name on the index card and tape the name to the other person. Instruct kids to refer to one another for the rest of the lesson by their new names.

Ask: • How could having different names help God's people forget about their lives in Jerusalem?

• How would you feel if someone changed your name without asking?

• How could forgetting about their pasts distract them from remembering God and his goodness?

Say: The next thing that Daniel and his friends had to do was learn the language of the Babylonians. They also had to learn all the important stories of the Babylonian culture.

Ask: • Have any of you had to learn a foreign language such as Spanish or French? Was it easy or hard?

Say: Daniel and his friends studied the language and the stories of Babylon. They probably had to spend a lot of time reading and learning.

Ask: • How could spending time doing homework distract you from remembering God and his goodness?

Say: They never stopped remembering God and his goodness. But the king had one more requirement. He wanted all God's people to eat his special food. But there were two problems: God had given his people strict rules about what they could and could not eat. Many of the king's foods were things that God's people were not allowed to eat. The second problem was that in those days, if you ate the king's food, it was a sign that you were giving your loyalty to the king. You were promising to give the king your loyalty and do what he thought was good.

Ask: • Why would this be a problem for God's people?

• Why would promising to give the king their loyalty make it hard for Daniel and his friends to do what they knew God thinks is good?

• What things can distract us from remembering God's goodness?

• What things help us remember God's goodness?

• How can spending time with God help us understand what it means to be good?

SCENIC ROUTE → Why not have a Daniel-style snack while discussing these situations? Serve a plate of carrot and celery sticks and some ranch dressing. If some of the children balk at the snack, use it as an opportunity to talk about how hard it might have been for Daniel and company to make the right choice while their friends dined on the rich foods of the king.

Say: Daniel convinced the king's servant to let them eat vegetables instead of the king's food. God honored Daniel and his friends. Just like Daniel, we can grow in our goodness by staying close to God and remembering his goodness.

ADVENTURES IN GROWING

(15 minutes)
Playing the Hand You're Dealt

Before class cut out the situation cards from a photocopy of "School Situations" (p. 67). Write the following Bible verse on newsprint or a board: "But just as he who called you is holy, so be holy in all you do" (1 Peter 1:15). Say: **We've been talking a lot about goodness. Everything good comes from God, because God is good. But there's another word to describe God's goodness: "holy." This verse challenges us to live holy lives, which is another way to say lives filled with goodness. But it's not always easy. Let's practice some ways to show goodness.**

Have kids sit in a circle. Set the deck of "School Situation" cards on the table. Invite a child to pick up a card, read it, and say how he or she would feel in that situation and what the right choice would be in that situation.

After each card has been drawn and each child has had a chance to respond, ask: • **Would it be hard for you to live out God's goodness in this situation? Why?**

• **Can you think of any other ways you could live out God's goodness in this situation?**

Say: **Sometimes it's easy to imitate God's goodness. Other times it's hard, just as it was hard for Daniel and his friends. But God wants us to imitate his goodness all the time. And God helps us, just as he helped Daniel and his friends.**

SOUVENIRS →

(10 minutes)
Goodness Served Here

Before class collect old food magazines. Scan the advertisements, and remove any that you feel would be inappropriate for young eyes.

Gather kids at a table. Provide paper, markers, safety scissors, glue, and pencils. Say: **Let's pretend that God has come to our restaurant. He's interested in seeing what kinds of goodness he can find on our menu. Write the words "Menu for Goodness" across the top of the page with a marker.**

Have kids browse through the magazines and cut out pictures of people who are doing good deeds. Have kids glue the pictures onto a sheet of copy paper. Next to each picture, have them write how that picture illustrates someone showing the fruit of the Spirit quality of goodness. Children will add their pictures to their Travel Journals.

HOME AGAIN PRAYER (5 minutes)

Say: **Look at your pictures of people showing the fruit of the Spirit quality of goodness. Circle the picture that represents how you want to show goodness in your life this week.** Give children a moment to choose how they plan to demonstrate goodness this week.

Have kids gather in groups of three or four and pray for opportunities to grow in goodness this week. After children have a few moments to pray, close by praying: **Dear God, you are good. ◗ We know we grow in goodness by spending time with you and thinking about your goodness. Help us to imitate your goodness. In Jesus' name, amen.**

TOUR GUIDE TIP

If kids have a hard time finding scenes of people doing good things, have them cut out people from different pictures and bring them together in a scene of their own making.

Items to Pack: pictures kids made in the previous activity, markers

FUN FACT

From 1991 to 1998 the Salvation Army raised 1.2 billion dollars to help people in needy situations. William Booth founded the Salvation Army in London, England, in 1878.

Cooking With Emerald

Emerald: Welcome to my number-one-rated cooking show in Babylon. Today on my show, we have a special honored guest. None other than Ashpenaz, the chief of all the King's court officials. Now chief, I understand that you have a special request for today's menu.

Ashpenaz: That's right. The king has ordered that I train some of the smartest young men from among the captives from Judah. I am to prepare these men to work for the king someday. There will be schooling...

Emerald: Schooling? So you want me to prepare some school cafeteria food? No problem! I will take some mystery meat, some lima beans, and Blammo! *(Pause.)* I will punch it up a level and have some great food!

Ashpenaz: I'm thinking a little classier than that. The king has ordered that these students eat the same foods and drink the same drinks that the king serves at his table.

Emerald: Blammo! *(Pause.)* I will have to punch it up! The king's food? Hmmm. Perhaps a fat, roasted pig with some leeks and garlic...some white wine...and dessert—maybe a rich, moist chocolate cake.

Daniel: We can't eat that!

Emerald: Hey! Quiet in the studio audience. This isn't interactive TV.

Ashpenaz: I recognize that voice...

Daniel: It's me, Daniel. *(Pause.)* My friends and I are some of the captives from Judah in your training. The king's offer to eat his food is generous. But God has told our people not to eat some of the foods that the king serves at his table. My friends Shadrach, Meshach, and Abednego all agree that we cannot do something that is not good in God's eyes.

Ashpenaz: I don't understand, Daniel. *(Pause.)* Your other friends from Judah don't seem to have a problem with eating the king's food...

Emerald: I should say not! I prepare nothing but the best. I am insulted. Ptouie on you, Daniel! *(Pause.)*

Daniel: *(Bowing)* Oh, great chief and chef—please do not be offended. I can't explain why no one else is refusing to eat the king's food. But we know what God expects from us. We must do what is good. Let us eat nothing but vegetables and drink nothing but water for ten days. After ten days, you decide who looks healthier—us or the students who eat the king's food.

Ashpenaz: But the king has his orders. I could get in trouble. Still, Daniel *(pause)*, I admire you for your courage to do what you know to be good, even when you could get in trouble. I don't understand why your God has this rule—but OK. I'll see you in ten days.

Emerald: Vegetables? Blammo! *(Pause.)* I will prepare you wonderful salads. I'll add a one-two punch to some eggplant. Maybe I'll make you an eggplant soufflé. Vegetables! I never thought of everything I can do with veggies.

Ashpenaz: *(To Daniel)* Remember, Daniel *(pause)*, I want to see you and your friends in ten days...

School Situations

Situation 1: Your best friend asks you to help him cheat on a math test. You want him to keep being your best friend. You could offer to tutor him, but that won't help him on this test. What do you do?

Situation 2: You saved your allowance money and did extra chores for weeks so you could buy that special toy. Your family is going to stop at the toy store right after church. Your Sunday school teacher announces that your class is taking a collection for a family who lost everything in a fire. You feel the wad of money in your pocket. What do you do?

Situation 3: Your teacher is sick. You have a substitute teacher. Everyone is acting badly and trying to get away with everything they can. You want to fit in. What should you do?

Situation 4: Everyone is picking on an unpopular kid in the class. If you are nice to this person, you might be picked on too. How can you show God's goodness to the unpopular kid and to your friends?

Situation 5: You are invited to go to someone's house to watch a video with a lot of violence in it. You really want to see it. However, you know that your parents would be very upset with you if you watched the movie. Why is watching the movie not a good thing to do? Can you think of another thing you and your friend could do together that would be fun for both of you and reflect God's goodness?

Situation 6: You've been busy all day and haven't had a chance to read your Bible or pray. You get a call from your friends. They want to go see a movie and invite you to come along. You know that goodness grows when we spend time with our good God. Think of three different ways you can handle this. Pick the best option.
1.
2.
3.

Situation 7: Your parents are tired, and they're taking a nap on the couch. They've asked you to be quiet while they sleep. Name five ways you can demonstrate God's goodness to them while they sleep. You may ask other kids to help you think of ideas.
1.
2.
3.
4.
5.

Situation 8: It's time for you and your sister to draw chores from the chore jar for the week. You are really lucky. You drew all the good chores while your sister drew all the nasty chores! Do you have opportunities to demonstrate God's goodness in this situation?

Faithfulness

Pathway Point: ⏺ You can count on me!

In-Focus Verse: "Let love and faithfulness never leave you; bind them around your neck, write them on the tablet of your heart" (Proverbs 3:3).

Travel Itinerary

Faithful people are solid, dependable, trustworthy, and reliable. Our children see many people break promises and not follow through on their word. Kids need to know that God calls us to be people of our word. Proverbs 3:3-4 exhorts us, "Let love and faithfulness never leave you; bind them around your neck, write them on the tablet of your heart. Then you will win favor and a good name in the sight of God and man." We can teach our children what faithfulness looks like and why it's important in their lives.

Faithful people can be counted on to do what they say they will do. They don't change their minds based on what other people think. We can all be faithful people by following what the Bible tells us to do. If we study God's Word and know what it says, we can make plans that please God and that we can carry out. Children will discover they can be friends whom others can count on.

TOUR GUIDE TIP

Explain the difference between leaning and pushing. Prayer is a time to quietly focus on the Lord, and you want to take care of any potential distractions before you start. Make sure that your helpers look for children who need buddies.

Items to Pack: blindfolds, objects for creating an obstacle course

DEPARTURE PRAYER (5 minutes)

One of the best ways children can learn to be faithful is through praying for one another's needs.

During the prayer, have kids choose buddies to put their arms around and to gently lean on.

Say: **Dear Lord, thank you that we can always lean on you. As we lean on each other, help us to remember that we can each be a friend to be counted on by praying for each other. Help us as we go through this lesson to learn how to be faithful people. Amen.**

1st STOP DISCOVERY (15 minutes) **Buddy Trust**

This game teaches kids to trust one another as they complete an obstacle course. They will see that to be counted on, a person must be trustworthy.

Have kids buddy up with the partners they had for the Departure

Prayer. If you have an uneven number of kids, a group of three will work fine for this game. Help children blindfold their partners. Say: **When we decide to be someone who people can count on, we need to be trustworthy and do what we say we'll do. Today, you're going to lead your buddy through an obstacle course without letting that person hit any objects in the course. Buddies, you are going to trust your partners who have given you their word that they will do as they say.**

Have the first pair line up at the beginning of the course. When the first pair is about halfway through the course, send the second pair through, and so on until all the pairs have negotiated the course. Then have partners switch roles and again go through the course. When everyone has played both roles in the game, gather children around you.

Ask: • **What was the hardest part about being blindfolded? Why?**

• **How did it feel to lead your buddy through the course?**

• **Was it better to be led blindfolded or to lead your blindfolded buddy? Why?**

• **Why is it sometimes so hard for us to trust?**

• **How does it make you feel when you are trusted?**

Say: **Being faithful is another quality of the fruit of the Spirit. Our game provided an opportunity to see what faithfulness looks like. A faithful person is someone who can be trusted. Faithful people will do what they say they'll do. You can count on them to be people of their word. Everyone, look at your buddy and in a loud voice say,** ⏱ **"You can count on me!"**

TOUR GUIDE TIP If the weather is nice, it's always fun to make an obstacle course outside. Be sure you have enough helpers to supervise the children. Set up the course before class so kids aren't waiting around. You can use the same objects you would use indoors, or you can use natural, outdoor objects such as branches or rocks to complete your course.

STORY EXCURSION (20 minutes)
Faithful Friends

In this activity, children will learn about faithfulness as a fruit of the Spirit quality. They will learn what it means to be faithful friends by looking at the example of David and Jonathan as told in 1 Samuel 20.

Items to Pack: worship songs, disguise for David (wig, glasses, hat, etc.), play spear, fake rock, play bow and arrows, table, two chairs

The setting of the play is your classroom. David is leading the worship songs for the children. Teach the children a new song that says, "Saul has slain his thousands, and David his tens of thousands"—1 Samuel 18:7b. The words can be chanted or sung to a tune. If available, tambourines are a nice addition. Kids will sing this song during the play.

Say: **The Bible tells us about two friends who understood faithfulness. Their names were David and Jonathan. Let's welcome our special guest who is going to help us lead worship today.**

David: My name is David. I am one of King Saul's generals and his personal harpist. I will be leading you in worship today. Have you guys seen Saul? I know that he's looking for me. I've been running and hiding from him. That's why I have this clever disguise with me. *(David shows kids his disguise.)* Now...no one let on who I am. I don't want him to kill me. *(David leads kids in singing worship songs.)*

(Allow for time for worship.)

(Saul periodically runs through the room during worship, looking for David and shouting. David puts on a disguise.)

Saul: Has anyone here seen David? I know that he's in here somewhere!

(The kids just keep singing. Then on the third time that Saul runs through the room...)

David: *(In disguise)* Oh yes, he went that away. *(Points to the door.)*

(Kids continue in worship.)

(Allow for time for worship.)

(Kids start singing "Saul has killed thousands, etc." Let them sing it at least three times all the way through, and Saul will interrupt them on the fourth time. Saul bolts into the room.)

Saul: *(Talking to the kids.)* OK! That's it! Stop singing right now! Yes, I have killed thousands. I have been your king for many years, and now all of a sudden, you all think that David is the best thing around! So he killed a giant—big deal—and a few thousand Philistines! Think about all the things I've done! I can't believe how quickly you people forget! David has taken all my respect. The only thing that he can take now is my kingdom! Well, you sing your little song. I'm going to go sharpen my spear. *(Saul leaves.)*

(After Saul leaves, Jonathan comes into the room.)

Jonathan: David! David! Where are you? David!

David: *(Takes off his disguise.)* Here I am, Jonathan.

Jonathan: You have to get out of here! My dad is looking for you, and he is mad!

David: Yeah, I know. He's really mad! I don't really understand it. I have done everything he's asked me to do. I have fought the Philistines. I have killed the giant, and I've even played the harp for him. The only thing I haven't done is let him turn me into a human shish kebab by not dodging his spear. What have I done wrong? Why does he want to kill me?

Jonathan: Oh no, David. He won't kill you. He tells me everything. He wouldn't hide this information from me.

David: Jonathan, he's already tried to kill me—twice! At least I'm fast on my feet so the spear missed me and hit the wall. He wouldn't tell you if he were trying to kill me—he knows that we're best friends and that you would warn me. He knows that we're as close as brothers.

Jonathan: Yeah, that's true. Well, what should we do? I don't want to lose you. I'll do anything.

David: OK, here's my plan. The New Moon Festival starts tomorrow, and I'm supposed to be there. Instead, I'm going to hide in the field until the evening of the day after tomorrow. If your dad notices that I'm not at the feast, tell him that my family asked me to come home for an annual sacrifice and that I asked you to let me go to my family. If he says, "All right," then I'm safe. But if he becomes angry, then you'll know that he's planning to kill me. Please do me this favor.

Jonathan: You are my best friend. I'll do anything for you. Now go, and I'll let you know how my father feels.

David: How am I going to know what to do? Let's make a plan.

Jonathan: OK, here goes. I'll wait until the day after tomorrow, and then I'll go out to the field. Why don't you hide behind those stones over there, and I'll come out with a servant to the field for target practice. I'll shoot three arrows. If I tell the servant, "Look, the arrows are on this side of you—get them," then you're safe and can come out of hiding. But, if I say to the servant, "The arrows are beyond you," then you're in danger and you need to leave because the Lord is sending you away. As for the promise that we have made to each other, the Lord will make sure that we keep it—brothers forever!

David: Brothers forever.

(They high five each other, and then David hides behind the rock. Jonathan leaves. After everyone has left the stage, Saul and Jonathan come back in and sit down for the feast.)

Saul: Man, this food is great! I do believe this is the best buffet we've had at one of these New Moon Festivals! Jonathan, my son, you're looking good this evening. Tell me, why has David not come to the feast either today or yesterday. Yesterday, I assumed that he was unclean, but that cannot be the case today. Where is he?

Jonathan: He begged me to let him go back to his family to have an annual sacrifice. I told him that it would be OK if he went.

Saul: *(Screaming)* What! How dare you tell him that he could skip this feast? Where is your family loyalty? Do you not love me? You've always sided with David and been a disgrace to me. Bring him here. He must die!

Jonathan: Why must he die? He has done nothing wrong!

(Saul picks up his spear and hurls it at Jonathan.)

Jonathan: AAAAAAHHHHHH! *(Runs out of the room.)*

(Saul stomps offstage, muttering about killing David. After Saul leaves, Jonathan enters the field and asks one of the kids from the audience to fetch arrows for him. David hides behind the rock.)

Jonathan: Run and find the arrows that I'm going to shoot.

(Jonathan shoots an arrow, then another. The child from the audience runs after the arrows.)

Jonathan: The arrow is farther on. Don't just stand there, hurry up! The arrow is beyond you. Here boy, please take these arrows back with you to town.

(The servant leaves, and David comes out slowly from behind the rock.)

Jonathan: I'm sorry. *(Starts crying.)*

(David bows to the ground three times then hugs Jonathan while crying.)

Jonathan: God be with you. The Lord will make sure that you and I, and your descendants and mine, will forever keep the sacred promise we've made to each other.

(They both leave the room, arms around each other.)

After the actors receive a round of applause for their excellent acting, say: **David and Jonathan loved God and each other. They were friends who knew they could be counted on. They were faithful. Let's look at some ways we can show the fruit of the Spirit quality of faithfulness.**

Items to Pack: masking tape, "Faithfulness" cards (p. 74), card stock

ADVENTURE IN GROWING

(15 minutes)
The Game of Faithfulness

Before class, copy the "Faithfulness" cards (p. 74) onto card stock and cut them apart.

As kids play this game, they'll learn to discern what a faithful person and an unfaithful person look like. Using the masking tape, tape off a room-sized game board to look like a Monopoly board. Make four corner squares and four squares on each side of the board. Kids will move around the board as dictated by the situations written on the "Faithfulness" cards. The goal is to be the first player to reach the end of the board. If the cards have all been used and kids are still playing, shuffle the cards and use them again. After the game, have kids talk about the experience.

Ask: • **What was it like to play this game?**

• **You moved a number of spaces after reading each card. Do you think the number of spaces you moved was fair? Why or why not?**

• Do these situations describe ways of being faithful? Explain.

• In what other ways can you be faithful?

Say: This game rewarded you for being able to say, "You can count on me!" In real life, we may not be rewarded for being faithful. But the fruit of the Spirit quality of faithfulness means being true to your word. Knowing that you were faithful in a situation pleases God. And that's the best reward we could have!

 (15 minutes)
Faithfulness Pictures

In this activity, children will draw themselves in faithful situations. Kids will add these pictures to their Travel Journals.

Have children form pairs and give each child a "Picture of Faithfulness" handout (p. 75) and coloring supplies.

Say: We've been learning about being faithful. These blank picture frames will give you an opportunity to draw a way to say, "You can count on me!" Write those words in the speech balloon on your picture now. Pause as children write the words. Say: Now talk with your partner and decide one way you can be faithful. After you've thought of something, draw a picture of you being faithful. You can both draw the same picture or create different ones.

HOME AGAIN PRAYER (5 minutes)

This prayer will give kids time to calm down before they leave and will give them time to reflect on what they've learned in class and how they can apply it to their lives. Pray: **Dear Lord, thank you for the fun we've had in class. We praise you that we can read the Bible and see examples of faithfulness in people who are just like us. Faithful people can be counted on. As we bow our heads, we'll now take a moment for each of us to pray to ourselves, not out loud, asking you to help us become more faithful in our actions. Let us tell you now that we're going to commit to being people who can be counted on.** (Allow a few minutes of silence.) **Thank you for telling us what we needed to hear today. Please be with us as we go through this next week that others will see our acts of faithfulness. Amen.**

ltems to Pack: crayons or colored pencils, 1 photocopy of the "Picture of Faithfulness" handout per child (p. 75)

FUN FACT
Did you know that dogs are called people's faithful friends? Dogs become attached to their owners, love them unconditionally, protect them, and help them. Dogs are used to guide the blind because they are reliable, steady, and trustworthy. Dogs can be counted on!

FUN FACT
Did you know that Monopoly has been sold as a game since 1935? You could say Monopoly fans are faithful followers of the game. And the longest Monopoly game ever played was 1,680 hours long—that's seventy straight days! (Now, *they're* what you call faithful Monopoly players!)

Faithfulness

Your friend at church helps you learn a Bible verse.

Move ahead 2 spaces.

You go to a birthday party, and your friend ignores you.

Move back 2 spaces.

Your friend takes time to help you study for a spelling test.

Move ahead 2 spaces.

You promised to return a book to the library, but you didn't.

Move back 4 spaces.

You told your friends you'd bring the football for the game, but you didn't.

Move back 3 spaces.

Your friend tells you about Jesus.

Move ahead 5 squares.

Your friend ignores you at recess and then apologizes.

Stay on your square.

You collect money for a fund-raiser, but you pocket some of it.

Trade places with someone behind you.

You promise your mom that you'll do your homework, and instead you watch TV.

Move back 2 spaces.

You see a friend doing something dangerous, and you tell an adult.

Move ahead 4 spaces.

A bully at school makes fun of your friend, and you walk away.

Move back 3 spaces.

You read your Bible every night.

Move ahead 5 spaces.

You share the story about Christ dying on the cross with someone.

Move ahead 6 spaces.

You make fun of someone for going to church so you won't be embarrassed around your friends.

Move back 6 spaces.

You give your Sunday school teacher chocolates for his or her birthday—you've just won the game! (Just kidding.)

Move ahead 1 square.

Permission to photocopy this handout from *Kids' Travel Guide to the Fruit of the Spirit* granted for local church use.
Copyright © Group Publishing, Inc., P.O. Box 481, Loveland, CO 80539. www.grouppublishing.com

Picture of Faithfulness

Gentleness

Pathway Point: ◐ God gives us gentleness to show the power of love without words.

In-Focus Verse: "See, your king comes to you, righteous and having salvation, gentle and riding on a donkey." (Zechariah 9:9b).

Travel Itinerary

Elementary-aged children understand the importance of being kind and sharing God's love with others. However, the way they show God's love is just as important as doing the action itself. To kids, gentleness is often associated with being weak or babyish. They're told to be gentle when petting an animal or when playing roughly with a sibling. But speaking one's mind and being powerful are more respected traits in the world around them. During this journey, kids will learn that gentleness is quite the opposite of weakness—it's God's power put into action with love. They'll discover gentleness is a trait that grows within us the closer we become in our relationships with Christ, because Jesus was the gentle expression of God's love put into action.

Younger children, who are still learning to control their emotions and who may have difficulty responding to situations with gentleness, will learn that gentleness is not always a response to others but an action to take toward others in love.

Some children are extremely shy during the elementary years and may feel discouraged about not being able to verbally share God's love with others. This journey will help kids understand that gentleness is a trait that quietly shows the power of God's love, and that God has equipped each of us with ears, arms, eyes, and mouths to speak the gospel of Jesus by living it with our lives.

TOUR GUIDE TIP If you have a large group of children, consider placing a large fan in the middle of your circle and simply observing its power.

Items to Pack: pinwheels

DEPARTURE PRAYER (5 minutes)

Gentleness is not a typical prayer request for children—especially in the terms they're used to when thinking of gentleness. Most people associate gentleness with being weak, soft, or timid. But the spirit of gentleness that God gives us is exactly the opposite—it's powerful, strong, and bold. Explain to kids that though it sounds backward, ◐ God gives us gentleness so that we can show the power of his love without words. Tell kids that God's love is gentle. Even though we don't hear it, we see it in action every day and it is a powerful thing. Give each child a pinwheel, or pass one around the circle. Lead children in the following prayer, having them stand together holding hands, with the pinwheel in one hand. At the end of the prayer, have kids hold up their pinwheels and blow them in unison.

Say: **Heavenly Father, we love you so much. We're sorry that we sometimes are not as gentle as you want us to be. Sometimes we speak too quickly or don't take the time to listen to others. We often try to tell someone about your love, Father, when that person needs to *see* it more than anything. Please grow your gentleness within our hearts, Father, and help us put our love in action. We pray that you would help us show people everywhere the power of your love and the strength of Jesus Christ—before we even speak a word. In Jesus' name, amen.**

(15 minutes) **Action!**

This activity demonstrates to kids that gentleness is an active trait, rather than a weak response to outside circumstances.

Before children arrive, write each letter of the word "gentleness" on separate sheets of paper. Place a piece of double-sided tape on the back of each piece of paper. Write the word "gentleness" on a chalkboard or large sheet of paper taped to a wall so children can check their spelling.

Choose five volunteers to come to the front of the room and sit in a row on the floor. Have volunteers close their eyes as you stick one sheet of paper with a letter to the bottom of each of their feet. If you have a large group, choose ten volunteers and tape one sheet to one foot of each volunteer. Say: **Today we're learning about the fruit of the Spirit quality God gives us called "gentleness." What images come to mind when you think of the word "gentleness"?** (Allow children to respond.) **Those are all great images. Often we think of things that are soft, cuddly, or delicate and dainty. When people tell you to be gentle, what do you normally think they want you to do?** (Allow children to respond.) **Often we hear that word when people want us to be careful with something, or to be calm or soft with something. But did you know Jesus was full of gentleness? And he was the most powerful person to ever walk the face of this planet! But he was *gentle* with people's hearts. He was strong and bold in his actions, but the way that he showed God's love was with quiet strength. That's what God's love is—it's an action that's so powerful it doesn't need to make a sound!**

Prophets proclaimed the power of Jesus many years before he was born;

SCENIC ROUTE ➞ If time allows, set up a table with plastic drinking straws and wadded-up pieces of paper or pingpong balls. Let kids have fun racing one another by using the straws to blow their own paper ball or pingpong ball from one end of the table to the other. Emphasize the power of their breath through the straw and how that is similar to how God breathes his power through each of us.

Items to Pack: paper, marker, double-sided tape, watch with a second hand

yet they knew they would recognize him by his gentleness—God's powerful love in action. Read aloud Zechariah 9:9.

Say: **Right now we're going to play a game to see whether we can work together to create "gentleness" without saying a word. Our volunteers have a letter on the bottom of each foot that spells part of the word "gentleness." However, the letters are all mixed up! The volunteers will have to move their feet around and arrange them so that the letters are in order to spell the word correctly. But the trick is, they can't say a word while they do it!**

Choose a timekeeper to time the group of volunteers to see how fast they can arrange their feet. Remind volunteers to look at the word written on the board or paper to help them know how to spell it. When they've finished, choose another set of five volunteers to race against the clock. Continue until each child has had a turn. You may want to allow some children to go twice if you don't have even groups of children.

Say: **Wow! You all did such a great job! You were all super fast and got your letters all switched around—and you didn't even have to say a word. I definitely saw a lot of action to make the word "gentleness"—and that's what gentleness is all about. It's quietly putting God's love in action.**

Have kids form pairs or trios to discuss the following questions:

Ask: • **What are some ways you can quietly put God's love in action?**

• **When has someone shown gentleness to you?**

• **How did it make you feel when someone was gentle in his or her actions toward you? Why?**

Say: **Gentleness is a powerful thing.** 🕐 **God gives us gentleness to show the power of love without words. We can be gentle by being polite to others and by thinking of others before ourselves. We can help others when they need something, listen instead of talking, and learn from other people. Jesus showed us what gentleness looks like, and it's our job to follow his example.**

SCENIC ROUTE If kids do well with this activity or if it seems too simple for your group, provide a challenge for them by writing out Galatians 5:22-23a, one word per sheet of paper, and have kids arrange their feet to put the verses together.

Items to Pack: eighteen-inch piece of thin wire per child, plastic-foam packing peanuts, Bible, small plastic adhesive bandages

STORY EXCURSION (20 minutes)
Hearts Ty-ed Together

In this activity, children will listen to a story and identify the ways gentleness is demonstrated.

Give each child a pre-cut, eighteen-inch piece of thin wire. Set out a box filled with plastic-foam packing peanuts. Read aloud 1 Kings 19:12-13.

Say: **The Lord came to Elijah in a gentle whisper.**

Ask: • **What does that tell you about God's character?**

• Do you think that when God wants you to do something he's going to come into your life and totally wreck your world in a loud and destructive way? What do you think he will do?

• How should we tell or show others about God's love? Why?

Have children string the packing peanuts onto their pieces of wire, making sure to leave about an inch of space at one end of the wire. When children have finished, have them form a heart shape with the wire, twisting the two ends together. Set out some small plastic adhesive bandages.

Read the story on pages 83-85 to the class. Instruct students to listen carefully. Each time kids hear of someone doing a destructive act—something the opposite of gentleness—children should use their fingers to crush one of the packing peanuts on their wire hearts. When they hear about a quiet act of love or gentleness, have them place a small plastic adhesive bandage on one of the crushed packing peanuts. The story begins with two acts of kindness, so have kids put bandages on the first two uncrushed peanuts. As the story progresses, kids will be able to find enough crushed peanuts to bandage.

If time allows, you may want to provide other materials for kids to use to decorate their wire hearts, such as ribbons, markers, glitter glue, or stickers. Display hearts in your classroom, in a window if possible.

After the story, have kids form pairs or trios and answer the following questions:

Ask: • What is gentleness?

• After hearing this story, in what simple ways can you try to show gentleness to others?

• Looking at the heart you've made, why do you think gentleness is such an important thing to God? Why does he want us to show gentleness to one another?

ADVENTURES IN GROWING

(15 minutes)
Show How You Grow

Children will act out actions of gentleness.

Items to Pack: sheet of butcher paper, marker, tape

Say: God gives us gentleness to show the power of love without words. It's a quiet strength. Think of how you feel when people are in your face yelling at you, bullying you, or trying to get you to do something. God has given each one of us a job to do, and that's to show others what his love looks like. The way he wants us to show others that love is through gentleness. Often we don't even have to say a word to others—we speak our love for Jesus' gift on the cross through the way we live our lives.

Right now we're going to divide into two teams and act out different ways to grow gentleness in our everyday lives.

Help students form two teams. Have each team choose a volunteer. Whisper

TOUR GUIDE TIP

You may want to allow volunteers from each team to come up with their own situations that reflect gentleness and add them to the class list.

one of the following gentle actions to both volunteers, and together have them act out the situations for their teams. Remind them not to say a word but to work together and let their actions do the speaking. See which team can guess first the situation being acted out. Rather than keeping track of points, choose a volunteer to keep track of the children's answers, listing them on a sheet of butcher paper, taped within their view.

- Smiling at or being friendly to someone who seems lonely
- Letting someone else go first to ride your new bike
- Letting someone borrow your pencil when his or hers breaks
- Sharing your lunch with someone who forgot his or hers
- Listening to someone else's problems
- Comforting someone who is hurting
- Learning from someone else's experiences
- Being excited with someone and sharing their joy at getting a good grade
- Being sad with someone who is sad about losing the soccer match
- Letting someone know you don't like what that person is doing without getting angry

SOUVENIRS (15 minutes)

Gentle Me

Children will write or draw ways they can use different parts of their bodies to show others the power of God's love.

Items to Pack: pens or pencils, photocopies of "Gentle Me" (p. 82), list from previous activity

Provide pens or pencils and a photocopy of the "Gentle Me" handout (p. 82) to each child.

Say: 🌑 **God gives us gentleness to show the power of love without words. God has given each of us the equipment—the various parts of our bodies—to use to show that power. Use a pen or pencil to write or draw ways you can use each of the parts shown on your page to show gentleness to someone this week.**

Hang the sheet of butcher paper with the list of gentle actions from the previous activity in a place where the children can see it. Encourage kids to look at it for ideas.

Say: **Because our God is the almighty, all-powerful God, he could've easily forced all of us to worship him. He could have screamed it in our faces, smacked our hands when we made mistakes, or shaken our shoulders and said, "You *will* worship me!" But that's not how God's love works. Instead, God showed us his love so that we would *choose* to worship him. God showed** us the power of his love by sending his Son, Jesus, to come to earth and teach us how to live. God showed us the power of his love in a gentle way. And that's exactly how God wants us to show others what his love looks like. He gave us ears to listen to people, eyes to cry with those who are sad or to see the needs of those around us, mouths to smile at strangers with, and hands to give hugs or pat someone on the back or help friends up when they're down. Just as God showed us his gentleness through his Son, Jesus, we can show that same power of God's love when we learn about and follow Jesus.

Items to Pack: Bible

HOME AGAIN PRAYER (5 minutes)

Have kids sit down. Open your Bible once again, and read 1 Kings 19:12-13. Have kids bow their heads and pretend to pull cloaks over their faces as you pray. Tell children to be absolutely silent at the end of the prayer and listen for God to whisper into their hearts ways they can be gentle this week.

Pray: Heavenly Father, we love you and thank you for the fruit of the Spirit quality of gentleness. Thank you, God, for giving us everything we need to quietly show the power of your love. Thank you, God, for showing us what gentleness looks like by sending your Son, Jesus, to walk on the earth and to die on the cross for our sins. Please help gentleness grow inside our lives, giving us hearts filled with your love. Help us listen to your gentle whisper speaking to us about the different ways we can share your love with others. Thank you for hearing and answering our prayers, Father. In Jesus' name, amen.

Allow a minute of silence.

Gentle Me

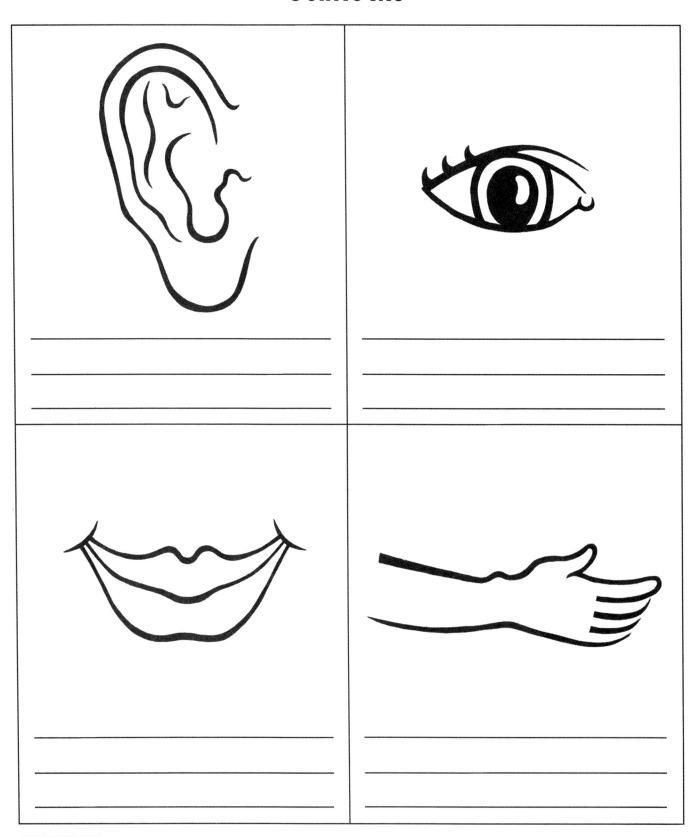

Permission to photocopy this handout from *Kids' Travel Guide to the Fruit of the Spirit* granted for local church use.
Copyright © Group Publishing, Inc., P.O. Box 481, Loveland, CO 80539. www.grouppublishing.com

Hearts Ty-ed Together Story

Even though Ty could normally think of about a billion other places he'd rather go to than school, he couldn't seem to get there fast enough today.

"Hey! Cool scooter, Ty!" shouted Thomas from across the playground as Ty rode up. (Each child should place a bandage on a packing peanut.)

"Whoa! You got it!" Mara squealed as she ran over to greet Ty. (Each child should place another bandage on a peanut.)

Kids began coming from every direction to check out Ty's new scooter.

"You sure are lucky, Ty! I can't wait till I have my birthday."

Ty beamed from ear to ear as he stared proudly at his sleek, silver, Lightning Edge scooter. His friends began pawing at the handle, trying to climb on for a ride.

"Hey!" shouted Ty. "Hands off! You're all getting your paw prints all over it! I had to wait an entire year for this beauty, and I don't want you guys messing it up!" (Each child should crush one of the peanuts.)

"But Ty! We just wanna take it for a spin!" whined Haley.

"Yeah! You're just being mean," Philip chimed in.

"Yeah!"

"Yeah!" the others complained.

Lucas walked up calmly and stared Ty straight in the eye. "New scooter?" he asked. (Each child should place another bandage on a peanut.)

"Lightning Edge—it's the best," Ty replied.

"Can I test it?"

"Not a chance." (Each child should crush one of the peanuts.)

"Why not?!" Lucas barked.

"Cuz you'll break it, that's why not!"

"You *are* mean—not to mention, a jerk! I'll just remember this when I get my new Play Center 3 game system. Don't even ask. A game system is ten times better than a stupid ol' scooter any day!" (Each child should crush one of the peanuts.)

"Stupid?! Who are you calling stupid?" Ty growled, pushing his scooter aside. (Each child should crush one of the peanuts.)

"Maybe the person who's too selfish to let anyone ride his stupid scooter—that's who!" Lucas snapped, stepping in closer. (Each child should crush one of the peanuts.)

"Fight! Fight! Fight! Fight!"

Mr. G heard the chanting coming from the playground and left behind the papers he was grading. As Mr. G approached the boys, he could see a flurry of arms and legs in a whirlwind of dust. The rest of the children scattered off to their respective playground positions while Mr. G picked Lucas and Ty up by the arms, dusted them off, and walked them into the building. (Each child should place another bandage on a peanut.)

Detention. Right after lunch, Ty and Lucas watched longingly through the window at the other kids playing kickball outside. A glint of silver metal—Ty's scooter—lay propped alone against the side of the building.

"It's all your stupid fault, ya know," Ty muttered under his breath. (Each child should crush one of the peanuts on the wire.)

"My fault? You wouldn't let anyone try out your scooter!"

"Exactly—*my* scooter. I had to wait all year for my birthday to come so I could get it. You've got a birthday. Tell your own parents to get you one!" (Each child should crush one of the peanuts.)

The room got eerily quiet, and Lucas lowered his head onto his arms folded on his desk. "Not such an easy task," he finally replied. "My parents are splitting up, and my Dad's moving to Texas."

Ty didn't know what to say. Sure his own dad went away on business trips sometimes—even to Texas once in a while. But he always came back. "Stinks to be you," Ty half laughed before turning back to look out the window. (Each child should crush a peanut.)

After school, Ty propped his new scooter against the pantry door and set his backpack beside it. Ty's mom came into the kitchen shortly after, her arms filled with grocery bags. She dropped her briefcase, which had been dangling by a few fingers, and she set the bags on the kitchen table.

"Hope you had a better day than I did, Ty," she muttered. "Anything exciting happen at school today?" (Each child should place another bandage on a peanut.)

"Um...just this," Ty mumbled as he handed the teacher's note to his mom. Ty tried to read the expression on his mother's face as she read about his fight at school. Was she angry? Was she sad? What was the punishment going to be? Ty hoped she would just yell at him and get it over with. But of course, she didn't. Instead she stared at Ty and dropped her hands to her sides. She looked...not sad...not really angry...what was it? Disappointed! That's it—she was disappointed. Ty's stomach sank. The words she didn't say were so much more powerful than if she were to simply yell at him. (Each child should place another bandage on a peanut.)

"Go to your room, Ty Regis Jr.," she finally spoke. "Now."

Ouch! The full name! Not the full name. Ty knew he was in trouble—big time. And he knew it would get even worse when his dad got home.

A pillow flew across the room just missing Ty's head the instant he opened his bedroom door. "Thanks, Jamen," Ty grunted as he flung himself onto the lower bunk. Jamen's head peeked over the upper bunk railing to see what was wrong with his little brother. (Each child should place another bandage on a peanut.)

"Ty—why so glum? You look like your dog just ran away or something."

Ty buried his head in his pillow and began to sob. "Everything went so wrong today! And it was supposed to be so great—I wanted to show all the kids my new scooter and all...and then I got the stupid note from my teacher...and now Mom's not talking to me, and Dad...and Dad...I don't even want to know!" The sobs grew louder.

Feeling a touch on his shoulder, Ty sat up to see Jamen sitting on the edge of his bed. (Each child should place another bandage on a peanut.) Jamen smiled at his little brother, and his eyes looked concerned. (Each child should place another bandage on a peanut.)

"Why don't you tell me exactly what happened." (Each child should place another bandage on a peanut.) So Ty told Jamen the entire story, about the scooter, about the fight, and even about Lucas' dad moving to Texas. Jamen didn't even have to say a word. It was just nice to have someone listen. (Each child should place another bandage on a peanut.)

When Ty had finished, Jamen quietly took off the shiny gold cross that he always wore around his neck and fastened it on Ty. "You're hurting now," he said. "But remember, Jesus knows all about hurt. And he hurt for you. You don't want to hurt other people. Your job is to love them and to tell them about the one that hurt for all of us—Jesus." (Each child should place another bandage on a peanut.) Ty thought about his friends, the scooter, and Lucas. Ty prayed for God to help him be gentle the next day.

The next morning, Ty was the first one to arrive at school. He waited by his scooter to let his friends take turns trying it out. (Each child should place another bandage on a peanut.) When his friends began to file onto the schoolyard, laughter and sounds of joy filled the air as they had fun taking turns on Ty's scooter. Lucas was the last one to arrive. He sat by himself on a bench and buried his head in his hands. Ty walked over and sat down. (Each child should place another bandage on a peanut.)

"I know you're hurting right now," Ty said, putting his arm on Lucas' shoulder. (Each child should place another bandage on a peanut.) "And I really am sorry about your dad." (Each child should place another bandage on a peanut.) Lucas looked up, amazed at the change he saw in Ty. "But I just want to show you something my brother gave to me," Ty continued. "It's a reminder that Jesus hurt, too. And he hurt for you and me. I also want to let you know that you're not alone, because God is right there with you feeling what you're going through. And...uh...I'm here for you too." (Each child should place another bandage on a peanut.)

Lucas used his sleeve to wipe off some runaway tears and smiled back at Ty. "Wanna check out my Play Center 3 game system after school?" he asked. (Each child should place another bandage on a peanut.) "My dad sent me one last night."

"You're on!" Ty smiled, and the two raced off to join the other kids.

JOURNEY 10
Self-Control

Pathway Point: 🌀 God wants each of us to practice self-control.

In-Focus Verse: "Be self-controlled and alert" (1 Peter 5:8a).

Travel Itinerary

To be self-controlled means to have power over one's outward reactions, emotions, and thoughts. In their toddler and preschool years, children often are not yet in complete control of their own emotions and actions. When they're hurt, they scream and cry, often uncontrollably. When they're angry, they often lash out at whoever or whatever is closest to them. Through training and guidance, they learn that uncontrolled reactions, emotions, and thoughts are unacceptable. The elementary years provide many opportunities for children to practice what they've been learning. They are now on their own for more hours each day, without the constant guidance of a parent or caregiver to help them make correct self-controlled responses. When they're angry, will they remember that hitting is not the correct way to deal with their anger? Will they put their initial desire for ten cookies aside and use restraint? Children who fail to learn self-control often end up hurt or hurting others. Their inability to put away their own selfish desires and wishes can cause mental, emotional, and physical pain for themselves or others. This lesson will help kids realize that 🌀 God wants each of us to practice self-control.

⚠️ **TOUR GUIDE TIP**

Before class write out the Departure Prayer on a piece of poster board, writing the words to be signed in bold, capital letters. Practice the signs several times so that you are comfortable and familiar with each sign.

During prayer time, point out each word to be signed and lead kids in practicing the sign several times. When kids are comfortable with the signs, read through the prayer together.

DEPARTURE PRAYER (up to 10 minutes)

It takes self-control to learn sign language. Encourage children to watch closely as you demonstrate each sign and then to follow along carefully as you sign the verse together.

Dear *Lord*, please prepare our *hearts*, our *minds*, and our *souls* as we study this lesson on *self-control*. Take all our *worries* and our cares; be with each one as we *share*. Amen.

Lord

hearts

minds

souls

self-control

worries

share

86

STOP 1st DISCOVERY

(10 minutes)
Blow 'Em Up and Let 'Em Go

This activity will help kids understand the difference between being in control and being out of control.

Items to Pack: balloons, pre-drawn bull's-eye target, tape

Before class, attach the bull's-eye target to the wall.

Give each child a balloon. Tell kids to blow up the balloons and hold them without tying them off. Instruct kids to let go of their balloons when you say "Go" to see what happens. Instruct children to keep a close eye on where their balloons go so they can find them and use them again. Have children blow up their balloons a second time and try to hit the target on the wall. Have kids throw away their balloons when they've finished this activity.

Ask children the following questions:

• **When you let go of the balloon the first time, could you predict where it would go? Why or why not?**

• **Were you able to hit the bull's-eye?**

Say: **When you behave uncontrollably, you're as unpredictable as our balloons were. No one knows what you may do or say at any given moment, just as we couldn't predict what our balloons would do. Today we're going to learn about the fruit of the Spirit quality of self-control. To have self-control means to be able to handle your thoughts, actions, and words and not let them do their own thing. We are going to learn why God wants each of us to practice self-control.**

TOUR GUIDE TIP

If you have several children who are unable to blow up balloons, consider pairing children so that one person is in each pair who can inflate the balloons. Have kids who know how to inflate the balloons do so and hand balloons to their partners.

STORY EXCURSION
(15 minutes)
In and Out of Control—the Story of Peter

Children will hear a first-person account from Peter's life and keep score of the times he is out of control and the times he shows self-control.

Items to Pack: pencils, paper

Give each child a piece of paper and a pencil. Have kids draw a line down the middle of the paper. On one side of the paper, have them write the words, "Out of Control"; on the other side, have them write "Self-Control." Tell children that they're going to listen to a story of Simon Peter's life. Each time the question "What do you think, out of control or self-control?" is asked, kids should make an X under the appropriate side. Each time children mark their papers, choose a couple of kids to explain their choices. Read the story as if you were Simon Peter.

Say: **Hello, my name is Simon Peter. I understand that you have been talking about self-control today. Many people who have read about my life say** that I was wildly out of control, making all sorts of crazy and foolish decisions. I must admit, I have not always used self-control and that has caused me some trouble in my life. But there have been times I practiced self-control and was able to make a huge difference. I'd like to tell you about a few times in my life and let you decide whether I was out of control or practicing self-control. When I first met Jesus and he asked my brother and me to come and follow him, I'm sure many people thought our going with him was an out-of-control decision. We left behind everything and followed him without knowing where we were going or what we were getting ourselves into. What do you think, out of control or self-control? (Have kids mark Xs on their papers.)

Then there was the time that I was in a boat with some friends and we thought we saw a ghost walking toward us on the water. We were really afraid, until we realized it was Jesus. Just to be sure, though, I yelled out to Jesus and told him, if it was really him, to tell me to get out of the boat and come. Sure enough, Jesus said to come. So I jumped out of the boat and started walking on the water. What do you think, out of control or self-control? (Have kids mark Xs on their papers.)

Once we were having dinner with Jesus, and he began to wash our feet. No way was I going to let Jesus wash my feet. You know what he told me? He said that if he didn't wash my feet, I would have no part of him. Well, I sure wanted to be a part of Jesus, so I told him to go ahead and wash my feet and my hands and head as well! Jesus informed me that I didn't need everything washed, just my feet. What do you think, out of control or self-control? (Have kids mark Xs on their papers.)

On the night that Jesus was arrested, I wanted so badly to protect him that I attacked one of the high priest's servants and cut off his ear. Luckily, Jesus put the ear back on and healed the servant. What do you think, out of control or self-control? (Have kids mark Xs on their papers.)

That same night, I did something I said I would never do. Three times I lied and told people that I didn't know Jesus. I got so angry that I yelled at the people who were questioning me. What do you think, out of control or self-control? (Have kids mark Xs on their papers.)

I'm so glad Jesus forgives! After his death, burial, and resurrection, he came to me and gave me another chance. He asked me whether I loved him, and I told him yes! He told me to go out and tell everyone about him, and I did just that. A few weeks later, a large crowd of people gathered and I gave the best sermon of my life! I used my words to tell them all about Jesus and how they could love him too. What do you think, out of control or self-control? (Have kids mark Xs on their papers.)

Another day I healed a man who had been crippled since he was born. Now don't get me wrong, I didn't heal him by my own powers, but by allowing the power of Jesus to work through me. What do you think, out of control or self-control? (Have kids mark Xs on their papers.)

Another time I had a dream that I should go and tell people who weren't Jewish, as Jesus and I are, all about the things he had done. I was about to argue with God, when someone came and asked me to visit a man named Cornelius. I couldn't believe it, he was one of these non-Jewish people. I wasn't too sure about this, but I obeyed God and went to see Cornelius. You know what I found out? Cornelius and his friends and family loved Jesus, too, and wanted to know more about him. Because I obeyed God, a whole bunch more people were able to find out about Jesus. What do you think, out of control or self-control? (Have kids mark Xs on their papers.)

I could tell you about so many more things. Sometimes I was out of control and sometimes I used self-control. I'll tell you this much, ◐ God wants all of us to practice self-control! Thanks for listening to my story, and remember that when you use self-control, good things can happen.

When you've finished the story, have children form small groups and answer the following questions:

Ask • What was the most out-of-control thing you think Peter did?

• What was the most self-controlled thing you think Peter did?

• In what ways are you like Peter? In what ways are you different from Peter?

Say: We all have times we are in control and times we aren't, just as Peter did. Let's practice ways we can allow God to give us more self-control in our lives.

SCENIC ROUTE → Instead of reading the story yourself, invite someone to your classroom, dressed up as Peter, to read the story to the children. Another option would be to videotape a volunteer acting out the story and then show it during your class time.

ADVENTURES IN GROWING

(15 minutes)
What to Do? What to Do?

Have children form four groups. Each group will act out an out-of-control situation and then will act out a self-controlled solution to the situation.

Before class photocopy the "What to Do?" situation cards (p. 92) and cut them apart.

Have kids form four groups, making sure to have a well-balanced number of older and younger children in each group. Explain to kids that you'll give each

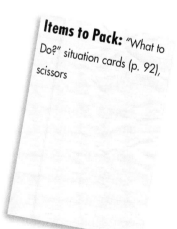

Items to Pack: "What to Do?" situation cards (p. 92), scissors

group a card that describes an out-of-control situation. They are to act out that situation and then come up with a self-controlled solution they can also act out. Give each group one of the "What to Do?" situation cards. Encourage group members to read through the card and then decide how they'll act out the out-of-control situation and then the self-controlled solution. Give kids five to seven minutes to prepare, and then bring everyone together and have each group act out its situation for the rest of the students. As children work, move around to each group and provide assistance where needed.

SOUVENIRS → (15 minutes)
Comic Strip

Children will make a comic strip based on 1 Peter 5:8-9a.

Before class, write 1 Peter 5:8-9a on a chalkboard or a sheet of newsprint. Also make photocopies of the "My Comic Strip" handout (p. 93) for each child.

Say: **In our story today, we learned about Peter. He did a lot of things that were out of control, but he did many things that showed he had self-control. Peter knew 🌓 God wants each of us to practice self-control. Peter knew how dangerous it can be if we don't practice self-control. In 1 Peter he wrote about what will happen if we don't have self-control. Let's read those verses together.**

Lead children in reading the verses from the chalkboard. When you have finished reading the verse, draw a dividing line after the following words: "alert," "lion," "devour," "him," and "faith." Write the numbers 1 through 5 over the appropriate section so children can find the right squares on their comic strips.

Say: **I'm going to give you a blank comic strip. I want you to fill in the squares with pictures that describe the Bible verse. I've divided the verse into five sections.** Point out the five sections on the board, and show the children how they correspond to the numbers on their comic strips. **For each section, you can draw or paste pictures from the magazines into the appropriate squares. When you've finished, please place your comic strip in your Travel Journal.**

Give children enough time to complete their comic strips.

Ask • **What does Peter say will happen to us if we don't practice self-control?**

Say: **The devil is always on the lookout for people who are out of control. He loves it when we do things that show we have no self-control. When we hit, punch, or kick; when we yell or swear; or when we want everything we see and don't want to wait, God is unhappy. That's why it's so important for us to remember that 🌓 God wants each of us to practice self-control.**

90

(10 minutes)

One Fruit

The children will compare an orange to the fruit of the Spirit.

Items to Pack: oranges, wet wipes

Have kids form groups of two or three. Give each group an orange, and tell kids to peel the orange but not to take apart its sections.

Ask • **How many types of fruit do you have in front of you?**

• **If you remove one section, how many types of fruit will you have?**

Have each group take out one section of its orange.

Ask: • **Is your orange a complete orange now?**

Say: **When we go to the grocery store and walk through the fruit sections, we'll see lots of different kinds of fruits to choose from. We can choose the ones we like and leave the others behind. We don't have to pick them all if we don't want to. But the fruit of the Spirit is not like that. It's not a bunch of different fruits that we can pick and choose from. It's one fruit with many parts. Each part is important to the other. The Bible says the** *"fruit* **of the Spirit is..." It is one fruit and we can't say, "I'll take love, joy, and peace, but leave patience and self-control behind." Just as our orange was incomplete when we took out one of the sections, our lives are incomplete if we don't work at having all the parts of the fruit of the Spirit.**

Allow children to divide the rest of the orange among themselves and enjoy a snack. As they eat their oranges, have kids try to list all the parts of the fruit of the Spirit. Encourage them to clean up their orange peels and wipe their hands and work areas with the wet wipes.

FUN FACT

Did you know that Charles Schultz, the creator of the comic strip *Peanuts*, drew the *Peanuts* characters for nearly fifty years and the comic strip appeared in more than 2,000 newspapers and in more than twenty-four languages?

HOME AGAIN PRAYER

(5 minutes)

Have children stand in a circle. Explain to them that when you're "on a roll," you're really doing a good job of something. Teach them the following cheer, and repeat it together several times, getting a little louder each time.

Say: **Self-control, I'm on a roll!** *(When you say, "I'm on a roll," roll your hands in front of your body.)*

After saying the cheer several times, close in prayer.

Pray: **Dear God, thank you for all the fun ways we've been able to learn about self-control today. Thank you that you are a God who will help us be in control. Amen.**

WHAT TO DO?

Justin and Alec were playing ball together at recess when Tyler came up and took the ball from them. Justin and Alec ran after Tyler, grabbed the ball out of his hands, and pushed him to the ground.

WHAT TO DO?

Carri and Emily were in their room listening to music. Carri wanted to listen to a new CD and put it in the CD player without asking Emily. Emily started screaming and yelling at Carri.

WHAT TO DO?

Jordan and Sarah were at the store with their mom doing the weekly grocery shopping. Every aisle they went down, one or the other asked for something. "Hey, Mom, can we have this?" "Hey, Mom, can we have that?"

WHAT TO DO?

The Sunday school classes were having a party, and everyone was looking forward to the pizza being delivered. When the pizza arrived, five of the kids ran up to the table and filled their plates to overflowing, leaving only three pieces for the other twenty kids who were there.

Permission to photocopy this handout from *Kids' Travel Guide to the Fruit of the Spirit* granted for local church use.
Copyright © Group Publishing, Inc., P.O. Box 481, Loveland, CO 80539. www.grouppublishing.com

My Comic Strip

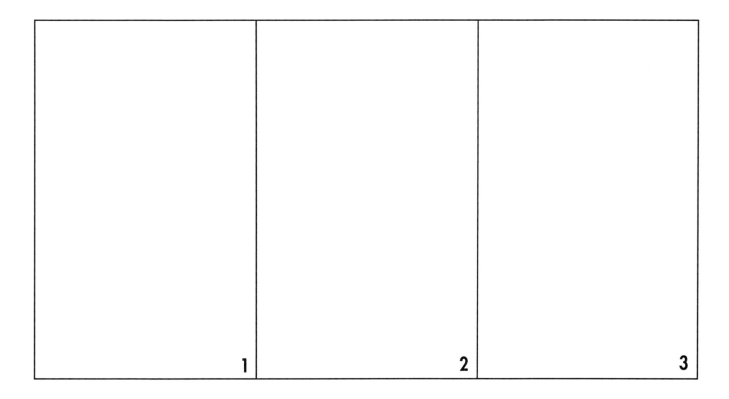

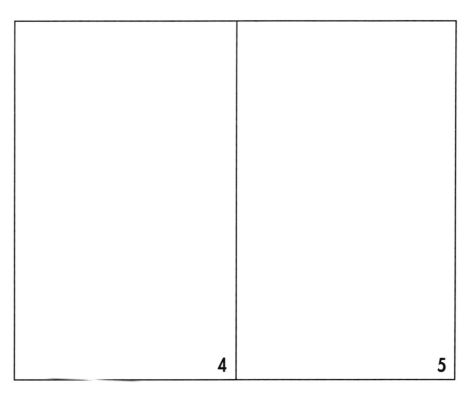

What It Means to Belong to Jesus

Pathway Point: ◑ When we belong to Jesus, the fruit of the Spirit is evident in our lives.

In-Focus Verse: "Those who belong to Christ Jesus have crucified the sinful nature with its passions and desires" (Galatians 5:24).

Travel Itinerary

When we accept Jesus as our Savior and become part of God's family, we become a new creation. As part of God's family, we need to begin to grow in our relationship with God. As we grow in that relationship, we should begin to exhibit traits that witness to our being God's children. In today's world, it isn't always easy to bear this kind of fruit and it takes the strength the Holy Spirit gives us to change our behavior.

As your kids grow and are challenged by the world, they need a reminder that they are God's children and must continue to bear his fruit. Colossians 1:10 says, "And we pray this in order that you may live a life worthy of the Lord and may please him in every way: bearing fruit in every good work, growing in the knowledge of God." This lesson will give you the opportunity to encourage kids to think about the various situations they face every day and how they can react to them in a manner that pleases God and bears his fruit.

Items to Pack: a current newspaper

| DEPARTURE PRAYER | (up to 5 minutes) |

In the world today, we don't always see people bearing God's fruit in response to situations that occur. Bring in a newspaper and discuss one or two current events, such as natural disasters or some kind of local controversy, and ask how we as Christians might respond and pray about these events. Ask two or three of your students to pray about something in your community.

Pray: **Dear Lord, thank you for loving us and giving us the gift of your Holy Spirit. Help us to use the power your Holy Spirit gives us as we live every day. We would like to pray specifically for** [allow students who are praying for your community to pray]. **Help us respond to our neighbors in a way that pleases you and lets them see you in us. Thank you for helping us. Amen.**

TOUR GUIDE TIP

When choosing news articles, be sensitive to the ages of your children and the magnitude of the events. Your examples need not be overly intense to be effective.

1st STOP DISCOVERY (10 to 15 minutes)
What's My Fruit?

This game helps children understand the characteristics of the fruit of the Spirit.

Items to Pack: Bible, address label stickers, pen, chalkboard, chalk

Before class, write on each sticker one fruit of the Spirit quality: love, joy, peace, patience, kindness, goodness, faithfulness, gentleness, and self-control. Make sure you have one sticker for each child. If you have more than nine children in your class, it's fine to double up on the qualities.

Read aloud Galatians 5:22-23a. List the fruit of the Spirit qualities on the board.

Have kids line up with their backs facing you. Go down the line and place a "fruit" sticker on each child's back. Have kids try to guess the names of the fruit of the Spirit qualities on their backs by asking yes-or-no questions of the other students. They could ask questions such as "Could I be considered happy?" or "In a tense situation, would I be OK?" or "If someone were getting on my nerves, would I lose my temper?" As soon as a child guesses a fruit of the Spirit quality, have the child put the sticker on the front of his or her clothing.

After all kids have figured out what fruit of the Spirit qualities they have, ask:

• **Was it easy or hard for you to figure out what fruit of the Spirit quality you had?**

• **Which qualities have similar characteristics?**

• **Do you understand how someone with your gift would behave?**

STORY EXCURSION (15 minutes)
The Tryouts

Say: **When we become Christians, we show others we belong to Jesus in how we act and react to different situations. We can react to most situations in a variety of ways. If we want to exhibit the fruit of the Spirit in our lives and show the world that we belong to Jesus, we will choose to react in a manner that bears his fruit.**

Read the story on page 99 to the class. As you read the story, stop at the places in the story that ask questions about Kyle's responses to the various situations he is in. Let your students discuss Kyle's responses at these times, and then continue with the story.

After the story, have kids form groups of three to answer the following questions:

Ask: • **In which of Kyle's situations was it the most difficult for him to exhibit the fruit of the Spirit? Why?**

• **Name one of Kyle's situations in which you would have reacted differently. Why?**

SCENIC ROUTE →

Bring in several different kinds of fruit to make a fruit salad to share. Ask:

• **What is your favorite kind of fruit?**

• **Would you like to eat only one kind of fruit all the time?**

Show kids your assortment of fruit. Assign each child a fruit to cut up. Have kids place the cut fruit in one large bowl. Say: **All of us have a specific fruit that is more natural for us to exhibit. Just as some of you cut up a banana and others cut up an apple, some tend to be more patient and others more kind by nature. But when we put all these fruits together, we have a delicious, healthy treat. As we produce all the qualities the Holy Spirit has made available to us and helps us with, we will be well-rounded, mature Christians. We can all be yummy fruit salads!**

• Can you think of a situation this past week in which you could have reacted differently and would have been more pleasing to God.

Say: **It's not always easy to let God's fruit be evident in our lives. But as we mature as Christians, these things will become more and more second nature, and we'll do them naturally.** ◕ **When we belong to Jesus, the fruit of the Spirit is evident in our lives.**

ADVENTURES IN GROWING

(15 minutes)
Fruity Situations

Before class, photocopy on card stock the nine "Fruity Situations" cards on page 100 and cut them apart.

Divide the class into three groups. Give each group three of the "Fruity Situations" cards. Ask each group to read its cards and come up with two responses to each of the three situations. Group members' first response should be their natural response, and the second will be the response the Holy Spirit would want them to give if they were exhibiting the fruit listed on their card. The two responses could be the same, or they may be quite different. Allow your class six minutes to do this. After six minutes, gather all the children, and have each group share its cards and how the group would react in each situation.

After each group has shared, say: **Our natural responses to many of these things are quite different from the way the Holy Spirit would have us act. But over time, as we allow the Holy Spirit to be more and more a part of our lives, exhibiting the fruit of the Spirit becomes a way of life. Through daily prayer and studying God's Word and letting it become a part of our lives, we can bear the fruit of the Spirit in our everyday lives.**

(10 minutes)
From Fruit to Light

Pass around a basket that holds an equal number of apples, oranges, and bananas. Make sure to have one piece of fruit for each class member. Divide the class into three teams. Those who choose apples will be together, those who choose bananas will be together, and those who choose oranges will be together.

Before breaking into your teams, together as a class read Galatians 5:24.

Give each team a flashlight. Have the apple team look up Ephesians 5:8, have the orange team look up Matthew 5:16, and have the banana team look up Romans 12:12. Turn out the lights in your classroom, and make the room as dark as possible. One by one, ask each group to turn on its flashlight and have a volunteer read its verse to the class. When each group has read its verse, turn on the lights in the room and come together as a class.

Ask • In the completely dark room, how noticeable was the light?

• How did you initially react to the light?

• How does the world react to someone who bears the fruit of the Holy Spirit?

Mosaic Fruit
(15 minutes)

Children will create a mosaic of the place they need God's help in being a light for him and bearing the fruit of the Holy Spirit. Kids will add these pages to their Travel Journals.

Items to Pack: white construction paper, bowls, one-inch squares of construction paper in many different colors, glue sticks

Give each student a piece of white construction paper and a glue stick. Have bowls of one-inch squares of construction paper in many different colors available on the tables.

Say: **During our day-to-day lives, we need to exhibit the fruit of the Spirit. This isn't always easy because we are imperfect and not always able to react as we should. In some places we go, it's harder than in others to bear the fruit of the Spirit. Maybe, for you, it's hard to show self-control at school. Or maybe you have a tough time being kind to someone at home. You know which places you need God's help in being a light for him. Create a mosaic of the place you need God's help in bearing his fruit. As you create your picture, pray silently for God to help you.**

Canned Fruit
(15 minutes)

This experiment will show kids which fruit of the Spirit qualities are most evident in their lives and which are not.

Items to Pack: masking tape

Before class, use the masking tape to make a large square in the middle of your floor. Make sure the square is large enough for at least half of the class to fit inside while standing. Tell kids the square is your can of fruit.

Have kids sit on the floor around the outside of the square. Say:  **When we belong to Jesus, the fruit of the Spirit is evident in our lives. Let's see how.** The object is to see how much fruit they can squeeze into the can. You're going to see which fruit of the Spirit quality is most likely to fill the can.

List the fruit of the Spirit qualities, saying one at a time. After you mention each quality, ask kids who've had the opportunity in the past week to show it in their lives to stand up and go to the center of the square. Let each person in the square give a brief description of the situation that allowed him or her to "produce" that quality. For example, for joy, a child may tell about being given an assignment in class that was very difficult. The child chose to do the assignment without making a fuss and actually ended up enjoying it and learning from it. Or for patience, maybe a child's little brother wanted to play a new game with the child, but the little brother wasn't very good at it. The child chose to help the little brother without getting angry as he was learning the game. After each quality, count how many kids are in the can and keep a tally. Then have those standing in the square sit down. Start over with the next part of the fruit of the Spirit. After all fruit of the Spirit qualities have been mentioned, check the tally sheet to see which produced the most full can and which the least.

Ask: • **Which fruit of the Spirit quality is easiest for you to exhibit?**

• **Which is hardest?**

• **Which do you have the most opportunity to exhibit?**

HOME AGAIN PRAYER (5 minutes)
Assign one gift of the fruit of the Spirit to nine different children in the class. If you have fewer than nine children, assign some kids more than one gift. As you pray, when it comes time to name the different gifts, go around the prayer circle and have the children say their assigned fruit of the Spirit gifts.

Pray: **Dear God, thank you so much for loving us and for sending us your Son and your Spirit. Help us to let the world know that ⬧ we belong to Jesus by the fruit that we bear. Help us to show** [have kids say the names of the gifts, one at a time] **in our lives. In Jesus' name we pray, amen.**

The Tryouts

"Kyle, be sure to keep track of your brother while you're at the ball field," Kyle's mom said as they left through the back door.

Kyle gave his mom the thumbs up as he placed his cap over his curly brown hair and jumped over the last three steps and off the back porch.

"You better be sure to stay with me and not go running off," Kyle said to his brother Jared as he gave him a little shove. (How could Kyle show *kindness*?)

As they approached the ball field, Kyle's heart began to race. It was going to be tough to make the team this year. At twelve years old, Kyle had not quite caught up with some of his friends, who all seemed to have had a growth spurt in that past year. He knew he had the abilities to be a good player, but he just didn't seem to match up when it came to size and speed. (How could Kyle obtain *peace*?) "Dear God, it's just you and me. I know you can help me do my very best while I'm out there," Kyle prayed as he signed in on the tryout list.

"Do you want to play catch with me while you wait for your turn? Maybe I can help!" Jared offered while tapping his own mitt. The last thing Kyle wanted was nine-year-old Jared's help.

"Sure, we'll go behind the bench until they call my name." Kyle figured it couldn't do much harm, and saying no would just make Jared cause a scene. (How could Kyle show *patience*?)

"Don't throw too hard. Sometimes you hurt my hand," Jared said as Kyle began to wind up. (How could Kyle show *gentleness* to Jared?) Kyle knew his friends were watching him. He wanted to just smack one in there, but he knew better. (What choice should Kyle make to show *self-control*?)

"Hey, Kyle! I'm glad you're here." It was Kevin, the new kid who moved in down the block from Kyle during the winter. He was kind of awkward, but a nice guy. "The glove my mom got me for the tryouts isn't really broken in yet. Is there any way I can borrow yours when it's my turn?" Kyle looked at his perfectly broken-in glove and thought a moment. (What should Kyle decide if he wants to show *goodness*?)

"I guess so. I hope it brings us both good luck!" Kyle replied.

Kyle heard his name called for his tryout. As he performed all the activities, he prayed all the while that God would help him do his very best. At the end of the day, when it came time for the coach to read the names of the kids who had made the team, Kyle heard his name. (How do you think Kyle responded to his feeling of *joy*?)

"If you are to be part of this team, I need to be able to count on you to make it to every practice possible. We work together as a team and to do so, we need everyone here. Can I count on you?" the coach asked the boys. (What should Kyle's response be if he wants to show *faithfulness*?)

As Kyle walked home with Jared, he was so excited about the prospects of the coming season. Jared could hardly keep his eyes off his big brother. Maybe someday he, too, could be on the baseball team.

When they arrived home, their mom was waiting with a fresh plate of brownies and a hug for them both. Kyle couldn't have been happier with the outcome of the day. He even gave his little brother a friendly squeeze as they went back out to their yard to practice ball. (How did Kyle show *love*?)

Fruity Situations

1. **Love:** A new girl is in your class. She is very quiet and always eats lunch by herself. You've seen her looking at you and your friends at recess. How could you show *love* to her?

2. **Joy:** Your Sunday school class is having a workday at your church. You've been asked to help pull weeds from the large flower beds in front of the church. You very much dislike pulling weeds. How can you show *joy* as you help out.

3. **Peace:** Your grandma is very ill. What can you do to have *peace* about what will happen to her?

4. **Patience:** Your three-year-old cousin is visiting. You're trying to put together a new puzzle that you've just received as a birthday present. Your cousin really wants to help. How could you show *patience* as he tries to help?

5. **Kindness:** Suppose you are at a friend's birthday party and one guest is being excluded from most of the activities. How could you show *kindness* to this person?

6. **Goodness:** You've just earned ten dollars by helping your neighbors clean out their garage. What could you do with your money that would show you had the fruit of the Spirit quality of *goodness*?

7. **Faithfulness:** An elderly next-door neighbor has asked you to help her by walking her dog every day for the next four weeks while her sprained ankle heals. It was fun in the beginning, but now it's been raining and you don't feel like you have much time. How would you show *faithfulness* in this situation?

8. **Gentleness:** Your friend's little brother has been bugging you and your friend all day. He sticks his tongue out at you and is just plain obnoxious. Your friend wants to hit him. If you want to show *gentleness*, what should be your reaction?

9. **Self-control:** You are at the mall with your mom. A new video game you've been wanting is on sale. You ask your mom whether she will get it for you, and she says no. If you wanted to show *self-control*, what would you *not* do?

Living by the Spirit

Pathway Point: ⬤ Living by the Spirit means not living by the sinful nature.

In-Focus Verse: "Since we live by the Spirit, let us keep in step with the Spirit" (Galatians 5:25).

Travel Itinerary

Every day things around us tempt us. Sometimes in big ways and sometimes in very small ways, we are tempted to lie, cheat, be unkind, or disobey. Temptations often influence our attitudes even if they don't affect our actions. Children aren't impervious to these temptations. Sometimes they feel them even more strongly than we do. Galatians 5 speaks a lot about the difference between living according to the Spirit and living according to the sinful nature. The products of each are detailed at the end of the chapter. Living according to the sinful nature produces more and more sin. But living by the Spirit produces the fruit of the Spirit in our lives. Children often have difficulty looking far enough down the road to see how their day-to-day decisions will affect their lives. We need to help kids see the repercussions of their potential actions. As our children face temptations, we need to help them make decisions to live by the Spirit, not according to their sinful natures. As Galatians 5 points out, living by the Spirit will lead to the wonderful fruit of the Spirit!

| DEPARTURE PRAYER | (up to 5 minutes) |

Have children sit in a circle.

Say: **Today we're going to learn what it means to live by the Spirit. You've been learning about the fruit of the Spirit and how important it is in our lives. Today we'll learn that to see this fruit in our lives, we need to live by the Spirit. In other words, when we do things God's way and follow God's direction, we'll see the fruit of his Spirit in our lives. It's a lot like following in another person's footsteps. If you follow in someone's steps, you do what they do. Following the Spirit's steps, or keeping in step with him, leads you to do what the Spirit would do.**

Have children remove their shoes and place them on their hands. Have them take turns "walking" their hands across the center of your circle while praying that God will help them learn to keep in step with the Spirit.

Say: **Dear God, please help us learn today what it means to keep in step** with your Spirit. Help us know how to follow you. We praise you, and we love you, Lord. Amen.

1st STOP DISCOVERY (15 minutes) Walking in Step

By practicing walking in another person's footsteps, kids can learn about keeping in step with the Spirit.

Have children form pairs.

Say: **We're going for a walk, but this is a special walk. The taller partner will walk normally. You can walk in a straight line, in curves, around obstacles, over things, or in whatever way you can think of. The shorter partner will follow the taller partner, trying to get his or her footsteps to land** *exactly* **where the taller partner's feet stepped. Experiment with walking closely and then walking a bit behind your partner.**

Take kids outside the classroom, and begin your walk. After a few minutes, have partners exchange roles and allow time for partners to walk as before in their new roles. Take opportunities to distract kids by talking to them individually. Return to the classroom and sit in a circle.

Ask: • **Was it hard or easy to follow your partner?**

• **Was it harder or easier when you were closer? farther away?**

• **Was it harder or easier when I was talking to you?**

• **How is this activity similar to or different from keeping in step with the Spirit?**

Say: **When you kept your eyes closely on your partner, it was easier to follow him or her. When we keep our minds and hearts focused on God, it's easier to follow what he wants for our lives.** ⬤ **Living by the Spirit means not living by the sinful nature. Let's all keep our eyes on God so we can live to please him.**

STORY EXCURSION (15 minutes) Decisions and Dilemmas

Kids will perform a simple narrative play to learn more about what it means to live by the Spirit.

Have a student or several students read aloud Galatians 5:16-17.

Ask: • **What is the sinful nature?**

Say: **Each of us is tempted to do things that are against God's ways. This is called our sinful nature.**

Ask: • What does living by the sinful nature mean?

• How does living by the sinful nature differ from living by the Spirit?

Say: It's important for us to understand what it means to live by the sinful nature because this is the exact opposite of living by the Spirit. 🌑 Living by the Spirit means not living by the sinful nature. Each time we're tempted to do something, we can ask ourselves, "Is this something that would please God's Spirit?" If the answer is no, your sinful nature is probably tempting you. And if you're living to please your sinful nature (if you're saying yes to those temptations), then you're not living by the Spirit. Let's do a simple read-aloud skit to emphasize the difference between living by the sinful nature and living by the Spirit.

Form three groups, and have children sit with their groups. One group will be the "sinful nature," one the "Spirit," and one the "Deciding Christian." Read this narrative aloud. Each time you point to the different groups, have them say these statements and do these actions: Kids in the Spirit group will say, "Follow me and you'll be fruitful," as they form halos over their heads with their hands. In an evil tone while rubbing their hands together, kids in the sinful nature group will say, "Follow me and you'll get what you want." Deciding Christians will say, "Oh, which do I do?" while throwing their hands in the air. Have children remove their shoes and place them on their hands. During the story, each time kids hear the word "walk," have them pretend to walk their shoes on the floor in front of them.

Say: **One day Deciding Christian went for a *walk*. As he strolled down the lane, he passed many people. As he passed one sweet older lady, he noticed a twenty-dollar bill drop from her purse onto the street. Suddenly, Deciding Christian's head was filled with thoughts. His sinful nature said,** [point to the sinful nature group to say its part]. **Then the Spirit said,** [point to the Spirit group to say its part]. **Then Deciding Christian said,** [point to the Deciding Christian group to say its part]. **After a moment, Deciding Christian reached for the twenty-dollar bill and handed it to the older woman. She thanked him, and Deciding Christian was on his way, feeling filled with more kindness and goodness.**

Ask: • What are some examples of kindness or goodness in our lives?

Say: **Let's hear more about Deciding Christian. On his *walk*, Deciding Christian thought he'd go see a movie. There were four movies playing at the theater: one was a movie his mother would not let him see. But his mom was not with him now. Then his head again filled with thoughts. His sinful nature said,** [point to the sinful nature group to say its part]. **Then the Spirit said,** [point to the Spirit group to say its part]. **Then Deciding Christian said,** [point to the Deciding Christian group to say its part]. **Deciding Christian** decided to see one of the movies that was OK with his mom. Suddenly he felt more peace and self-control.

Ask: • What are some examples of peace and self-control in our lives?

Say: Let's hear what else happened to Deciding Christian. After buying his ticket, Deciding Christian received the wrong change. He had received change for a twenty when he had paid with only a ten-dollar bill. He had ten dollars too much! Then his head again filled with thoughts. His sinful nature said, [point to the sinful nature group]. Then the Spirit said, [point to the Spirit group]. Then Deciding Christian said, [point to the Deciding Christian group]. Deciding Christian handed the cashier the extra ten-dollar bill, and the cashier thanked him. The cashier nearly cried when he realized the mistake he had made but was so relieved by Deciding Christian's honesty. Deciding Christian's heart then filled with faithfulness and joy.

Ask: • What are some examples of faithfulness and joy in our lives?

Say: Deciding Christian *walked* into the theater and sat down. As he waited for his movie to begin, Deciding Christian realized that each time he had been tempted by his sinful nature, he had been wise enough to choose to live by the Spirit, *not* by his sinful nature. As a result, the fruit of the Spirit increased in his life.

Ask: • Have you ever had your head filled with thoughts like these? When? Tell your group.

• What did you end up doing? Tell your group.

• If you chose to keep in step with the Spirit, can you think of any ways your life was changed because of your good choices? Tell your group.

Say: God hopes that we'll make choices to keep in step with his Holy Spirit. He knows that it's for our best to live this way. 🌀 Living by the Spirit means not living by the sinful nature. When we choose to live according to the Spirit, we grow closer to God and become more like him. His personality begins to show more in our lives, and we begin to exhibit the fruit of the Spirit.

SCENIC ROUTE → Form groups of four. Photocopy the "Decisions and Dilemmas" skit (pp. 103-104), and hand out one copy to each group of four. Have each group practice its skit and take turns performing the skit for the whole group. For added creativity, have the groups choose new statements for the Spirit, the sinful nature, and Deciding Christian to say.

Items to Pack: bottle of bubbles with bubble wand, basket, yellow construction paper, scissors

ADVENTURES IN GROWING

(10 minutes)
Bubble Bonanza

Children will follow bubbles across the classroom and try to attain the fruit of the Spirit.

Before class, cut several banana shapes from yellow construction paper, and place them in a basket. Place the basket of "bananas" at one side of the room, and gather children at the opposite end of the room.

Say: After I blow a batch of bubbles, choose one to follow as it travels through our room. Your goal is to follow the bubble to the basket of bananas. Keep in mind that you may not fan or blow your bubble. You may only follow it.

Ask: • How easy or hard do you think this will be? Why?

Blow enough bubbles for each student to have one to follow. Blow more bubbles if needed, giving children several chances to get across the room to the fruit basket. As kids follow the bubbles, they may notice that their bubbles are *not* leading them to the basket of bananas. This is the idea. They're learning that following the bubble, like following our sinful nature, does not lead us to a Spirit-filled life.

Ask: • Where did your bubble lead you?

• Did your bubble lead you to the basket? Why or why not?

Tell children that the rules of the game are changing. Now they are to follow *you* across the room to the bananas. Lead kids across the room to the basket. Make it fun, adding twists and turns as you lead them. After each student has reached the basket, have children sit in a circle.

Ask: • Did I lead you to the basket of bananas?

• Which was the more reliable way to the basket, following me or following the bubble? Why?

• Which is the more reliable way to see the fruit of the Spirit in your life, by following your sinful nature or by following the Spirit? Why?

Say: Following the bubble is like following your sinful nature: We wander around but don't really get to where God wants to lead us. But when we live by the Spirit and keep in step with the Spirit, as when you followed me, we begin to see the fruit of the Spirit in our lives.

(20 minutes)
Role-Play Reactions

Children will role-play different situations in which they make choices to live by the Spirit.

Before class photocopy and cut apart the "Role-Play Reactions" cards (p. 109).

Have children form groups of four. Give each group a situation card. Ask kids to read the card, assign roles, and practice acting out the scenario. After the groups have had about five minutes to work out their role-plays, have each group take a turn performing its situation for the rest of the class.

Ask: • How did it feel to choose to live according to the Spirit?

• Were you tempted to choose to live according to the sinful nature? Why or why not?

SCENIC ROUTE → Cut enough bananas for each student to have one. Write one fruit of the Spirit gift on each of the bananas, and put them in the basket. When students reach the basket, have each student choose a banana and take it to discussion time. After the discussion questions, ask each child to describe what his or her gift means.

SCENIC ROUTE → To spice up this activity, place a fan in the corner of the classroom so the bubbles move about more actively.

Items to Pack: photocopy of "Role-Play Reactions" cards (p. 109), scissors

TOUR GUIDE TIP

If you have more groups than situation cards, make extra copies and give the same situation card to more than one group.

Items to Pack: masking tape or yarn

• What does it mean to live according to the Spirit?

Say: 🌑 Living by the Spirit means not living by the sinful nature. It means choosing to live your life the way God wants you to live it. When we live our lives this way, to please God, we become more and more like him. As we do that, the fruit of the Spirit becomes more and more evident in our lives.

(10 minutes)
Spiritual Circles

Children will play a game that illustrates how close to or far away from God we can get based on the decisions we make in life. They'll learn why it's so important to live according to the Spirit.

Find a large area to play this game. Make a series of five concentric circles on the floor with masking tape or yarn (or even chalk if you do the activity outside). The smallest circle should be about five feet in diameter, and each successive circle should be about two feet wider in diameter than the one before.

Say: We're going to play a game to see how our decisions affect how close to or far away from God we can be. In our daily lives, we make decisions: little decisions and big decisions. We make some of these decisions influenced by the Spirit and some influenced by our sinful nature. Think about this as I read you a story.

Stand in the center of the smallest circle, and have children stand on the nine-foot-wide circle and spread out evenly. Read the narrative below.

Say: Once upon a time, there lived a kid named Pat. Pat loved to go in-line skating. One day Pat's mother asked her to give the dog a bath after school, and before she went skating with her friends. Pat didn't want to take the time to wash the dog because her friends could only skate for the next forty-five minutes. Anyhow, she could wash the dog after she skated, and her mother would never know the difference. What would you do if you were Pat? Be honest! If you would wash the dog first, take a step to the next smaller circle. If you would go skating with your friends and wash the dog later, take a step to the next larger circle.

Before dinner Pat wanted a cookie. Dad said no, but she still wanted one. She slipped into the pantry, grabbed the cookie, and quickly munched it. Unfortunately, she left crumbs on the pantry floor. When Dad asked her about it, she was tempted to lie. She could blame the crumbs on her little brother, who couldn't even talk to defend himself, or she could tell the truth, but probably get in trouble. What would you do? If you would blame your sibling, take a step to the next larger circle. If you would tell the truth and face getting in trouble, take a step to the next smaller circle.

Reach out your arms and twist from side to side as your arms gently swing through the air. Ask kids to try to touch your hands from where they're standing on their circles. Some will probably be able to touch you and some probably won't.

Ask: • How hard or easy is it to reach my hands? Why?

• If I, standing here in the center of the circle, represent God, how do the choices you made in our story influence how close to or far away from me you are right now?

• How is our game like real life?

• Why is it important to live according to the Spirit?

Say: In real life, when we make choices to walk according to the Spirit, we grow closer to God. But when we make choices to walk according to our sinful nature, we get farther away from him. ◐ Living by the Spirit means not living by the sinful nature. We can begin to see the fruit of the Spirit in our lives only if we're willing to live according to the Spirit. The more we walk according to the Spirit, the more we become like the Father. And the more we become like the Father, the more we will see the fruit of the Spirit in our lives.

SCENIC ROUTE → Instead of standing in the center of the smallest circle, place a small radiant heater in the center. Instead of asking the children to touch your hands, have them compare the warmth of the heater from close up and farther away. Explain that just as we can feel the warmth more when we are closer to the heater, so it is with God. We can feel his warmth and be more in tune with him when we make choices to walk according to the Spirit.

SOUVENIRS → (15 minutes)
Funny Footprints

Kids will make funny footprints to show the path they would choose to live by the Spirit. Kids will add these pages to their Travel Journals.

Items to Pack: nontoxic ink pads, baby wipes, photocopies of "Funny Footprints" handout (p. 110), markers

Before class photocopy page 110 for each child. Set out baby wipes to use for cleanup throughout the project and afterward.

Say: To show that we want to live by the Spirit, let's make footprints from the person on our page to the side of the page that says, "Living by the Spirit." You'll also color the person in the picture to look like you, to show that you are the one making the choice to live by the Spirit.

TOUR GUIDE TIP If you don't have ink pads, children may use markers to color their fists and fingers to make the footprints.

TOUR GUIDE TIP

If you don't have very many ink pads but have a large group, ask half the class members to color their people while the other half use the ink pads. Have groups switch supplies after five minutes.

Demonstrate how to make the footprints, using the diagrams for reference. Make a fist, and press it pinky side down onto the ink pad. Then press your fist on the handout for the first footstep. Press your index finger onto the ink pad, and use your inked finger to print toes along the top edge of your previously inked image. Have children continue this process, alternating hands to create left and right feet, until the footprints reach the words at the top of the page that read, "Living by the Spirit." Have children clean their hands with baby wipes, and then have each child color the person at the bottom of the page to look like himself or herself.

HOME AGAIN PRAYER (5 minutes)

Say: **Today we've learned that following our sinful nature can be similar to following bubbles. It gives us something to do but doesn't get us where God wants us to be. As I blow more bubbles, let's each take a turn popping the bubbles and saying this prayer.**

Blow one set of bubbles for each child to pop as he or she says this prayer.

Dear God, please help me to *not* follow my sinful nature but to follow your Spirit. Amen.

Role-Play Reactions

Situation 1:

A new kid comes to your school. She looks different from the other kids at your school. Your sinful nature wants to avoid her because she's different. The Spirit wants you to make friends with the new student. You choose to live according to the Spirit.

Situation 2:

You're playing on the playground at school. A bully comes by and steals your football. Your sinful nature wants to get even by stealing his lunch from his locker. The Spirit wants you to use your words to work out your problem. You choose to live according to the Spirit.

Situation 3:

Your neighbor has a new dog, and she has invited you over to play and see the new dog. You really want to go, but Dad has said that you may not because dinner is almost ready. Your sinful nature wants to beg, whine, and complain until you get your way. The Spirit wants you to accept your dad's decision and work toward another chance to see the neighbor's dog. You choose to live according to the Spirit.

Situation 4:

You've been playing in the empty field behind the old grocery store and twist your ankle in one of the prairie dog holes. Your parents have forbidden you to play there because they believe it's not safe. When you get home from the field, your ankle is really hurting and getting red and swollen. Your sinful nature wants you to lie to your parents about where you were when the accident happened. The Spirit wants you to tell the truth, no matter what kind of trouble you might get into. You choose to live according to the Spirit.

Funny Footprints

Living by the Sinful Nature.

Living by the Spirit.

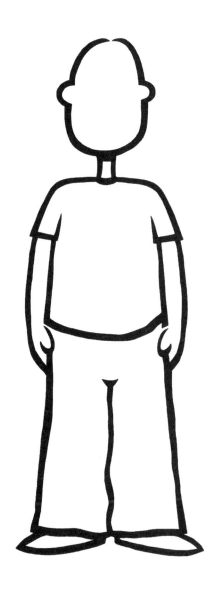

Staying With or Straying From the Spirit

Pathway Point:  God gives us fruit of the Spirit to help us learn what is pleasing to him and what is not.

In-Focus Verse: "Let us not become conceited, provoking and envying each other" (Galatians 5:26).

Travel Itinerary

It's important to teach our children that they're important, not because of their accomplishments but for who they are in God's eyes. But children this age face incredible pressure to fit in, and often those pressures lead kids to stray from following the qualities of God's fruit of the Spirit.

Provoking one another is a hobby for many children who are either bored or seeking attention. And envying others is a difficult part of human nature for children to fight when they struggle daily with being popular and being accepted by peer groups. During this journey, kids will learn that living lives pleasing to God doesn't necessarily come easily. God's will is often the opposite of what our sinful nature wants to do. But kids will also learn that the battle is the Lord's! By nurturing the fruit of the Spirit that God grows within us, God helps us to live to please him, rather than living to please others or ourselves.

| DEPARTURE PRAYER | (5 minutes) |

Children have already learned about the various gifts of the fruit of the Spirit, which God grows within each of us the more we know him. Now as kids focus on putting those traits into action, they will begin to discover how actions that please God don't necessarily come naturally—in fact, they are often in direct opposition to our human nature. Reassure kids that God will help those pleasing actions, or fruit of the Spirit, grow naturally the more we follow Jesus' example and walk in his footsteps.

Items to Pack: paper plates

Before children arrive, create a path of "footprints" made from paper plates. Run the path around your facility, outdoors, or wherever space allows. Be sure to space the paper plates to make it challenging for older kids. Lead children on a prayer walk. Kids will make a single file line and hop from plate to plate, alternating feet each time. As you pray, remind children to keep quiet and listen, and one at a time, have them fill in the blank at the end of the prayer with a fruit of the Spirit quality they would like to see God grow strong in their lives.

Say: **Heavenly Father, we love you so much. We know that we don't always**

SCENIC ROUTE →

If you're in an environment that allows it, take children on a prayer walk outside. Encourage them to think of ways they can show fruit of the Spirit in their lives toward God's creation, such as showing love to their environment by picking up trash and keeping it clean, showing the patience to grow flowers rather than pick them, and so on.

Items to Pack: Bible

TOUR GUIDE TIP

Select volunteers to demonstrate what being conceited, provoking someone, or envying someone means. This will help the children who are more visual learners better understand the definitions of each word.

do the things that please you. But Father, we know that you help us do what is right by growing the fruit of the Spirit in our lives. Help us, Lord, to walk in Jesus' footsteps and show others love, joy, peace, patience, kindness, goodness, faithfulness, gentleness, and self-control. Help us to not become conceited, angry, or jealous. Instead, especially grow [allow children to fill in the blank with a fruit of the Spirit quality] in our lives. In Jesus' name, amen.

1st STOP DISCOVERY Attitude Is Everything (15 minutes)

This activity demonstrates to kids how differently a situation can turn out as a result of our attitudes and actions. They'll observe the difference between actions that please God and actions that do not.

Read aloud Galatians 5:22-26, and say: **We've been learning a lot lately about the fruit of the Spirit. By now I think we understand pretty well what love, joy, peace, patience, kindness, goodness, faithfulness, gentleness, and self-control look like. Those are all behaviors that please God.** ☽ **God gives us the fruit of the Spirit to help us learn what is pleasing to him and what is not. The fruit of the Spirit helps us battle those bad, sinful behaviors that come naturally to us.**

Reread Galatians 5:26.

Ask: • **What do you think it means to become "conceited"?**

• **What does it mean to "provoke" someone?**

• **What does it mean to "envy" someone?**

Say: **Being conceited means that you think you're better than other people are. And when you provoke someone, it means you try to make him or her mad on purpose—you're teasing someone or showing off just to get that person's attention. And when you envy someone, it means you're jealous of that person. You want the things that person has more than you want the things that God has to offer.**

When we follow Jesus, we don't want that sinful part of ourselves anymore. We want to do what Jesus would do in every examples we face. Our attitudes are everything! Let's take a look at a couple of examples that will show us how differently one situation can turn out by changing our attitudes!

Have children pair up. Instruct pairs to choose one person to be a boy named Will and the other person to be a boy named Ned. Read the following situation to the children, and have them act it out several times in the various ways that you instruct them.

Say: Will and Ned are best friends. They have both decided to try out for the traveling soccer team. After tryouts, Ned finds out he has made the team, but Will hasn't. Ned is now going to tell Will the news. How will Ned tell Will? How does Will react? Let's see what happens if...

1. Ned tells Will with joy, and Will responds with joy.

2. Ned tells Will in a way to make him feel bad or to provoke him, and Will responds by being jealous.

3. Ned tells Will in a way that is full of conceit and acts as if he's better than Will, and Will responds with gentleness.

4. Ned tells Will in a very kind way, and Will responds with love.

5. Ned tells Will with joy, and Will responds full of conceit, thinking he's better than everyone else is.

6. Ned tells Will with love, and Will tries to provoke Ned to be mad or to feel bad.

Each time, choose several different pairs to perform their actions and reactions for the group. When children have gone through the different scenarios, ask pairs the following questions, calling on several pairs to share with the group as a whole.

Ask: • Which do you think was the best way for Ned to tell Will the news? Why?

• Which way do you think was the best way for Will to respond to the news? Why?

• Have you ever been in a similar situation? How did you behave?

Say: ◐ God gives us the fruit of the Spirit to help us learn what is pleasing to him and what is not. When we use the fruit of the Spirit to help us in difficult situations, we please God. When we are conceited, provoking, or envying in our actions, we are not behaving as Jesus would. We need to pray for God to help us in our actions, so that we can tell others what it means to be a Christian by simply behaving in ways that please our heavenly Father.

TOUR GUIDE TIP If you have a small group of children, simply call on various volunteers to come up before the whole group and act out each attitude scene.

STORY EXCURSION (20 minutes) Fruit Fight!

Before children arrive, use a masking tape line to divide your room in half. Set out a large pile of newspapers on the line.

Gather children in the middle of the room, and have them sit in a large circle. Say: **We've learned a lot about ways to behave that please God.** ◐ **God gives us the fruit of the Spirit to help us learn what is pleasing to him and what is not. But we've also learned that growing that fruit isn't**

Items to Pack: piles of newspaper, masking tape, Bible, fruit chew snacks always easy! Our first reaction to something may not be the way God would want us to behave. For example, you might "accidentally" let yourself become conceited if you get a lot of really cool gifts for your birthday. It would be really easy to let yourself think you were better than everyone because you had all that really cool stuff. It's hard to remember sometimes that the only thing good about each of us is the good that God has put inside us. Nothing we have—not the coolest clothes, the newest skateboard, or the trophies we win at Little League—makes us special to God. We're special to God already! Everybody repeat after me: I'm special to God! (Allow children to respond.) He made us! And he loves each of us so much that he sent his Son to die on the cross so we could be with him forever! So we need to live our lives in ways that please God—not living to please others.

The Bible also tells us not to provoke others and to try not to make others become angry or feel bad. I know sometimes we provoke others anyway, maybe because we forget or we get bored, or maybe we don't even mean to do it. But it's important for us to pay attention to the things we say and do so other people will see behaviors that please God.

Envying someone, or wanting to be like someone else—to be popular and have lots of friends—that's something we all feel sometimes. But you know what? There is only one person we should ever strive to be like. Shout out who that is! Lead kids in shouting out "Jesus!" Say: That's right! People make mistakes, because, well...because they're people. But Jesus was God's Son, and he was the only person who ever lived that never, ever did anything wrong. That's why we should want to be like Jesus and want what God has to give us, not what this world tells us we need to have. I know that's not an easy task. But God helps us!

There's a battle going on every single day we live. It's a battle between doing what we know God wants us to do and doing what we know God doesn't want us to do.

When Jesus walked on the earth, he told his disciples about the ways of God's kingdom. Those ways are not ways of this world. People at the time probably thought Jesus was crazy! But we know that Jesus spoke the truth to teach us how to please God. And that's what we need to focus on—not on how we can please people or how we can please ourselves, but on how we can please God.

Read aloud Matthew 5:1-12. Then say: Now those words might have seemed a little confusing to you. "Blessed" means "great happiness." And when we obey God's commands and live as Jesus taught us to live, by the fruit of the Spirit, God promises us great happiness!

Right now we're going to fight a battle to remind us of the battle we have to fight every day to live the way God wants us to!

Divide children into two teams, and have each team stand on either side of the masking tape line on the floor. Read aloud Galatians 5:26. Tell one team that its part of the verse is, "Let us not become conceited." The other team's part is, "provoking and envying one another." Divide the newspaper evenly, allowing children to wad up newspaper balls for their teams.

After each team has made its paper balls and when you give the signal, instruct teams to throw the paper balls over the line—as many and as fast as they possibly can. Explain that you'll give them several minutes to throw as many paper balls as they can onto each other's side, and that when you give the signal to stop, each team will count up how many paper balls they have on their side of the line. The goal is to have the fewest on your team's side when the signal to stop has been given. As children throw, each team should also call out together its part of the verse, back and forth from team to team.

Give children approximately five minutes to throw the paper balls from side to side. When you give the signal to stop, have kids count the paper balls to see which team has the most on its side. Then say: **Wow! You all did a great job fighting in battle today! Every day the world throws things at us, trying to attack us and make us do things that aren't pleasing to God. And whenever we feel like we're getting beaten by the world—like when we start to feel conceited, or when we provoke someone or envy others—you know what we need? More fruit! That's right—we need to pray for God to give us the strength to be more like Jesus and for the fruit of the Spirit to fill us.** Point to the team with the most paper balls. Say: **It looks like this team was really getting attacked! So let's fill them up with some more fruit!** Give prepackaged fruit chew snacks to the team with the most paper balls.

Say: **God knows each one of us needs fruit of the Spirit to grow in our lives. So let's give the other team some fruit, too!** Give prepackaged fruit chew snacks to the other team as well. Allow children to sit and eat their snacks as they answer the following questions:

Ask: • **How did it feel to have so many paper balls flying at you?**

• **Have you ever felt as if the world were throwing paper balls at you, trying to get you to do things that aren't pleasing to God? When?**

• **What did you do or what would you do differently next time?**

SCENIC ROUTE → Depending on the age and skill level of your children, consider setting out used sheets of copy paper, or old flyers that may be lying around your facility. Have kids make paper airplanes out of the sheets of paper. Have teams fly the planes onto each other's side instead of throwing the paper balls.

ADVENTURES IN GROWING

(15 minutes)

Check Yourself Before You Wreck Yourself

Set out a large flower box, or several large flower boxes if you have a large group of kids. Before children arrive, cut out nine round circles from construction paper, and write a different fruit of the Spirit quality on each circle—to represent seeds. Tape a piece of paper to the side of a watering can and write, "Good Stuff" on the paper. Have a bag of potting soil nearby.

Say: **Today we're learning what not to do when we're trying to live the way God wants us to.** Reread Galatians 5:26. Say: **So how do we not do those things?** 🕑 **God gives us the fruit of the Spirit to help us learn what is pleasing to him and what is not. The more we learn about Jesus, love him, and follow him, the more fruit we will see grow in our lives! So let's learn right now some different ways we can help that fruit grow to replace the conceit, provoking attitude, and envy that try to grow like weeds in our lives.**

Lead children to the flower box. Hold up the circles with the fruit of the Spirit qualities written on them.

Ask: • **Where does fruit come from?**

• **How does it begin?** Allow kids to respond.

Say: **Fruit starts from seeds! Let's all say the fruit of the Spirit qualities together as we plant them here in our fruit garden.** Lead children in saying, "But the fruit of the Spirit is love, joy, peace, patience, kindness, goodness, faithfulness, gentleness and self-control," as you set the "seeds" down in the flower box. Say: **These are the ways God wants us to show his love to others. So to grow fruit in our lives, we need to give these seeds what they need to grow. A good place to start is to bury ourselves in God's Word, the Bible. This is how God talks to us. The Bible tells us about Jesus—who he was, and what he did—so we can learn about him and know how we can follow his example. So let's pretend this soil is God's Word, and we'll bury these seeds in God's Word.** Cover the cutout seeds with potting soil. Then give each child an index card and a pen or pencil.

Reread Galatians 5:26. Say: **So for fruit to grow in our lives, the Bible tells us not to become filled with those bad things. What do you think we should fill ourselves with?** Allow children to respond, and then read Philippians 4:8. Say: **We need to fill ourselves with good things! Right now, I want you to write about or draw something you think is good or pleasing to God. When you've finished, place it in the watering can labeled "Good Stuff." When** each child has placed his or her card in the water, choose a volunteer or two to pour the water over the flower box.

Say: OK—so we've buried ourselves in God's Word. We've filled ourselves with things that please God. What else can we do to help our fruit grow? Allow children to take guesses. Say: Have any of you ever heard people say that talking to plants helps them grow better? Well, talking helps our fruit grow, too! We need to talk to God regularly. Give each child a second index card. Say: Let's talk to God right now by writing about or drawing something you want to tell God. When you've finished, plant the card in the soil to help the fruit grow!

When children have finished, bring out a big basket filled with seasonal fruit, such as apples or oranges. Then say: When we fill ourselves with good things, bury ourselves in God's Word, and talk to God regularly, our fruit will start to grow! And it's going to grow and grow and grow, until it's overflowing in our lives. So when we have all this fruit growing in our lives, all this—say it with me—love, joy, peace, patience, kindness, goodness, faithfulness, gentleness, and self-control, what should we do with it? (Allow children to respond.) God wants us to share it, to use it, to give it away. Remember, we learned a while back that the fruit of the Spirit helps others know what God's love looks like. And if we don't show them his love—the fruit of the Spirit—that's growing inside us, how will others know what his love looks like?

Give each child a piece of fruit and a blank adhesive mailing label. Have kids peel off the backings and place their labels on their fruit. Set out markers for the kids to share. Write out Galatians 5:26 on a chalkboard or on a large sheet of butcher paper attached to the wall. Instruct children to copy the verse onto their labels. When children have finished, whisper into each child's ear a different fruit of the Spirit quality, duplicating as much as necessary.

Say: God wants us to share the fruit of the Spirit with others instead of letting ourselves be filled with things that aren't pleasing to God. So think of the fruit of the Spirit quality that I've whispered to you, and think of a way you can give your piece of fruit to someone in the room, delivering it in a way that shows your fruit of the Spirit quality. For example, if you have the word "joy," you could jump for joy or shout "yippee!" all the way over to someone and give them your fruit. If your word is "love," you could hug someone before giving that person your fruit. Be creative!

When kids have finished delivering their fruit to one another, have them write their names on labels and add the labels to their new pieces of fruit. Have kids set aside the fruit to take home.

SOUVENIRS (15 minutes)
Attack!

Children will think about ways the fruit of the Spirit helps us not become conceited and helps us not provoke or envy one another.

Say: God gives us the fruit of the Spirit to help us learn what is pleasing to him and what is not. Today we've learned that becoming conceited, provoking one another, and envying one another are not pleasing to God. Something important to remember when you become a Christian is that you are in a relationship with God—just as you have relationships with all your friends at school. And when you're friends with someone and you know their very favorite things, such as their favorite flavor of ice cream, their favorite song, and their favorite color, you don't purposely go and give your friend everything he or she hates. You give your friends the things they like and treat them the way they like to be treated. That's exactly what God wants from us—to give him the things that make him happy. And nothing makes God happier than when we love him and all the people he's made.

God sent Jesus, his one and only Son, to come to live on earth and to show us the ways that make him happy. Not once did Jesus ever show conceit, try to make someone feel bad, or become jealous of other people. No! Jesus did only things that were filled with what? Lead children in shouting, "love, joy, peace, patience, kindness, goodness, faithfulness, gentleness, and self-control!" Provide a photocopy of the "Attack!" handout (p. 120) to each child. Say: Jesus is our example of how to live our lives to please God. So right now, take a look at the different situations on your Travel Journal page. For each picture, think of something you could do to show love, joy, peace, patience, kindness, goodness, faithfulness, gentleness, and self-control. Write which fruit of the Spirit quality you think would work best to make the situation better and what you would do to show that fruit.

HOME AGAIN PRAYER (5 minutes)

Have kids sit down. Open your Bible again and read Galatians 5:22-26. Say: When we belong to Jesus, we don't want that sinful part of ourselves anymore. We want to do the things Jesus would do. The cool part is, we don't have to worry about what to do—God grows the fruit of the Spirit in our lives the more we come to know him. Read Isaiah 64:8. Then tear off an eight-inch square of aluminum foil for each child, and give each child a small lump of self-hardening clay. Ask children to hold the clay on the foil while you pray, and then allow them to shape their clay into something that personally symbolizes what is pleasing to God.

Pray: **Heavenly Father, we love you and thank you for the gifts of the fruit of the Spirit. Thank you for helping us fight the battles against the world's ways. We know you are the potter and we are your clay. We want you to grow your love inside each of us and shape us into who you want us to be. Please help us stay away from doing wrong things, and give us the courage to do what is right. We thank you for Jesus and ask that as you grow the fruit of the Spirit within us, you will help us be more like Jesus each and every day. In Jesus' name, amen.**

Attack!

Permission to photocopy this handout from *Kids' Travel Guide to the Fruit of the Spirit* granted for local church use.
Copyright © Group Publishing, Inc., P.O. Box 481, Loveland, CO 80539. www.grouppublishing.com